W9-ABC-896

CHICAGO PUBLIC LIBRARY
THOMAS HUGHES
400 SOUTH STATE STREET
CHICAGO, ILLINOIS 60605

Rosalind Franklin

and the

Structure of Life

ROSALIND FRANKLIN

AND THE

STRUCTURE OF LIFE

Jane Polcovar

MORGAN REYNOLDS

PUBLISHING

Greensboro, North Carolina

R0409774707

CHICAGO PUBLIC LIBRARY
THOMAS HUGHES
400 SOUTH STATE STREET
CHICAGO, ILLINOIS 60605

Profiles

IN SCIENCE

Robert Boyle

Rosalind Franklin

Ibn al-Haytham

Edmond Halley

Marie Curie

Antonio Meucci

Caroline Herschel

Copyright © 2006 by Jane Polcovar

All rights reserved.
This book, or parts thereof, may not be reproduced in any form
except by written consent of the publisher. For more information write:
Morgan Reynolds Publishing, Inc., 620 South Elm Street, Suite 223
Greensboro, North Carolina 27406 USA

Library of Congress Cataloging-in-Publication Data

Polcovar, Jane.
   Rosalind Franklin and the structure of life / by Jane Polcovar.
      p. cm.
   Includes bibliographical references and index.
   ISBN-13: 978-1-59935-022-6 (library binding)
   ISBN-10: 1-59935-022-X (library binding)
   1. Franklin, Rosalind, 1920-1958--Juvenile literature. 2. Women
molecular biologists--Great Britain--Biography--Juvenile literature. 3.
DNA--History--Juvenile literature. I. Title.
   QH506.P65 2006
   572.8092--dc22
   [B]

                                            2006016864

Printed in the United States of America
First Edition

This book is dedicated to another woman of incredible energy and talent—my daughter, Lara Polcovar

Also, with daily gratitude and love, to my mother Paula Dunn (1923-2004)

Contents

Rosalind Franklin. (Courtesy of the National Portrait Gallery, London.)

ONE
EARLY YEARS

In his famous memoir about his groundbreaking work on DNA, *The Double Helix*, the geneticist James Watson describes his reaction, in January of 1953, at first seeing an X-ray image labeled Photo 51. "The instant I saw the picture my mouth fell open and my pulse began to race." He immediately recognized that the photo was proof of the helical structure of the DNA molecule. Watson and his partner Francis Crick had been preoccupied for months by the structure of the DNA molecule—one of the most important problems in science. The first scientists to make the discovery were almost certain to win a Nobel Prize, the world's top scientific honor.

Watson continued: "The pattern [in the photograph] was unbelievably simpler than those obtained previously. Moreover, the black cross of reflections which dominated the picture could only arise from a helical structure. . . . mere inspection of its X-ray picture gave several of the vital helical parameters. Conceivably, after only a few minutes' calculations, the number of chains in the molecule could be fixed." In other words, the X-ray image told him everything he needed to know to set him on the right track. The next day, Watson and his colleagues began working on a double helix model of DNA. Less than two months later, Watson and Crick would send a paper to the pres- tigious science journal *Nature* laying claim to be the first to discover the structure of DNA. In 1962, as expected, Watson, Crick, and Maurice Wilkins, the man who first showed Watson Photo 51, were awarded the Nobel Prize for medicine and physiology.

The scientist who had taken Photo 51 and other X-ray photographs critical to the unlocking of the DNA molecule was not on the stage in Stockholm, Sweden, to share in the Nobel Prize. Tragically, Rosalind Franklin had died four years earlier at the age of thirty-seven. She had gone to her grave never knowing how critical her work had been to one of the most famous scientific discoveries in history.

Rosalind Franklin's role in the discovery of DNA's structure would remain obscure for years. Ironically, it was the publication of Watson's bestselling book in 1968 that brought her to the attention of a wider audience and began a movement to see that she received more credit. Watson did not intend to make the case that Rosalind Franklin was the unsung hero of DNA. Throughout the book he jokes about the terrible "Rosy" who made life miserable for him and the other men who were working on DNA in the early 1950s. But it was his portrayal of her that led many to revisit her contribution to one of the most important scientific achievements of the twentieth century.

Rosalind Elsie Franklin was born on July 25, 1920, into a distinguished London family. The Franklins traced their lineage back to King David and up through generations of English and eastern European Jews. The family name was originally Fraenckel and had been anglicized to better fit into English society. Rosalind's family, like many other established English Jews, was a tight-knit but well assimilated group, renowned for their philanthropic activities. Rosalind's great-uncle Sir Herbert Samuel was the first practicing Jew to serve in a British Cabinet and was the first high commissioner of the British mandate of Palestine.

Rosalind's mother and father, Muriel and Ellis Franklin, had a loving, traditional relationship. Muriel, a kind, intelligent woman, willingly accepted her role as wife and mother. She usually echoed her husband's wishes and tended to the children. Muriel's aspirations for a university education had been thwarted by her mother's objections, but she found an outlet for her intellect and skills in charity work.

Ellis Franklin was an affable, opinionated man who expected to be obeyed. He had planned to study science at Oxford but after finishing his service as a captain in an infantry regiment during World War I, he married and began a career in banking. He worked at the Keyser

Bank, where his father was senior partner. He set aside his dreams to enter the family business and expected his wife and children to be willing to make similar sacrifices. The Franklins' five children arrived in rapid succession: David in 1919, Rosalind in 1920, Colin in 1923, Roland in 1925, and Jenifer in 1929.

The Franklins lived in wealthy West London, in the heavily Jewish Bayswater enclave, near Ellis's father and Muriel's parents. The families often dined together on Friday evenings. The Franklins moved easily through the wealthy and educated London society. Rosalind was raised in a manner typical of English girls of her class. She attended private schools and went away to boarding school for a time when she was nine years old. A much beloved nanny cared for her and her siblings on a daily basis. Rosalind took trips abroad with her family and developed a love for travel she kept her entire life. She was usually surrounded by relatives and peers of equal social standing.

Rosalind's grandparents were comfortable with their wealth. They owned several estates, including a country home complete with tennis courts, a five-car garage, an adjoining farm, and a large staff. Ellis Franklin, however, lived much less ostentatiously. He did not want a chauffeur and commuted daily to the bank by train. Although he could have afforded it, he never owned a second home. Nevertheless, childhood schoolmates of Rosalind who were invited to her home later recalled the grand life their school friend led.

According to the ethos of the Franklin family, with

wealth came a responsibility to give back to the community. Ellis volunteered as a teacher and later as vice-principal at an institution called the Working Men's College, which offered free university classes at night to men who worked as laborers during the day. He also taught at the college several evenings a week after working all day and sometimes did not get home until nearly midnight.

Young Rosalind with her doll pram. (Supplied by Churchill Archives Centre, Cambridge, © Jenifer Glynn)

The Franklins were, as a rule, an upright family not given to open displays of affection. They argued passionately about ideas but rarely discussed their emotions.

Rosalind, an intelligent, lively, and often unruly child, often felt slighted by what she saw as unequal treatment compared to her brothers. When quite young she became ill from an infection that left her weak and susceptible to further complications. Her parents put her on a program of restricted movement and forced naps, which she greatly resented, especially when her brothers were allowed to run free.

When she was nine, Rosalind's parents sent her to boarding school. Her mother felt that time at the Sussex coast, with its sea breezes and ocean air, would help Rosalind recuperate from her illness. Rosalind's sister, Jenifer, was born just as Rosalind was being sent away. Rosalind was heartbroken to have to leave. She wanted to stay at home with her nanny to play and help with her baby sister. The decision had been made, however, and she left for school.

Rosalind's prior schooling at Norland Place, a private day school in West London, prepared her for the academic rigors at Lindores School for Young Ladies. Lindores catered specifically to physically ill and weak children, but the academics were strenuous—even a notch above Norland Place. Rosalind was homesick her entire time at boarding school, but also thrived on the competition, earning high marks and accolades from her teachers.

Finally, in the summer of 1931, she was brought home

St. Paul's Girls' School still looks much the same today as it did when Rosalind attended. (Image Reprinted Courtesy of St. Paul's Girls' School.)

cured of her illness. Rosalind's illness and subsequent exile at boarding school would continue to loom large in her memory as acts of injustice. That Lindores catered to sickly children also greatly disturbed her, and she would, for the rest of her life, remain stoic in the face of illness or physical pain, ignoring it when possible and resenting it when it proved impossible to ignore.

In 1932, at the age of eleven, Rosalind's parents enrolled her at St. Paul's Girls' School. St. Paul's was a public day school in West London, a short bus ride from her home, with an excellent academic reputation and a progressive approach to education. Girls, though kept separate from the boys, were taught a similar curriculum and were encouraged to pursue careers.

The competitiveness and high standards of St. Paul's suited Rosalind. She soon discovered her love of science. "We spent the whole arithmetic lesson to-day with a lovely discussion about gravity and all that sort of stuff," Rosalind wrote to her parents. She liked sports and played tennis, hockey, and cricket; she also joined the Debating Society.

At one point the headmistress called in Rosalind's parents because Rosalind and her new best friend Jean Kerslake had been bullying Jean's ex-friend. "Rosalind and I achieved a certain notoriety which strengthened our alliance," recalled Jean, who would remain a lifelong friend. Even as a young child, Rosalind showed signs of the qualities that would later define her. She was aloof and shy around those she did not know well. Although she could be amicable, she became combative and cold when her defenses were up. Anne Crawford, another lifelong friend from St. Paul's, would later describe Rosalind as a "very private and strictly compartmentalized person."

Rosalind's cousin Ursula Franklin, who also went to St. Paul's, once saw Rosalind at a dance sponsored by the St. Paul's Girls and Boys Schools and noticed Rosalind's innocence when it came to the opposite sex. Rosalind arrived at the dance with Jean, each wearing a short party dress that made them look like children when everyone else was in floor-length gowns. No one asked them to dance the entire evening.

By the time Rosalind was fifteen, she knew that science was her passion and wanted it to be her career. She enjoyed the logic of scientific thinking and the adventure of experimentation. Science was also mostly solitary work, which suited her personality. St. Paul's had excellent science facilities and did not dissuade the female students from exploring this traditionally masculine field.

Rosalind was growing up during a very unsettling time. As Joseph Stalin and Adolf Hitler consolidated power in the Soviet Union and Nazi Germany during the 1930s, waves of Jewish immigrants fled to England, further stressing an economy already buckling from a worldwide economic depression. Some Britons resorted to anti-Semitism out of fear that the Jewish immigrants would take their jobs. At the same time, many established English Jews took measures to relocate the refugees.

Rosalind's parents threw themselves into refugee relief work. Ellis cut his hours at the bank and at the Working Men's College to help the Home Office issue entry permits for fleeing refugees. St. Paul's permitted Rosalind and her classmates to be released early from school to help with refugee paperwork and filing.

Some Austrian Jews were so desperate to save their children from Hitler that if they themselves could not leave Austria, they packed their children onto a network of trains, called the Kindertransport, which arrived weekly in

As Adolf Hitler's Nazi Party grew in power, few observers failed to notice that Germany was preparing for war. Europe began to observe one other disturbing fact: Hitler's rhetoric was no longer merely philosophical, the regime had begun to put anti-Semitic laws into action. (Library of Congress)

London. Nearly 10,000 children came to England without homes or relatives to care for them.

Ellis became involved in finding placements for these children. The Franklin family took two children into their home. A nine-year-old girl named Evi Eisenstadter came to stay in 1938 and became good friends with Rosalind. When she arrived in England, Evi was met by the chauffeur, who drove her to Rosalind's grandfather's country estate where the family was spending the weekend. When Evi first saw the grand setting and Rosalind's well-dressed grandfather walking down the imposing front staircase, Evi thought he was the king of England.

two

YOUNG RESEARCHER

Franklin was eager to leave St. Paul's to pursue a higher level of scientific study. When she was seventeen, she took the entrance examinations at Cambridge in physics and chemistry. Although she worried that she had not done well, Franklin placed first in the chemistry exam and was offered admission to both Girton and Newnham Colleges, the two women's colleges at Cambridge University. She decided on Newnham.

Ellis Franklin was not sold on the idea of his daughter entering college to study science. A college education that prepared her for child rearing and maybe social work was one thing; professional education was entirely different. His daughters did not need to work in any profession, much less one with such limited opportunities for women.

He proposed that she pursue social work, as so many

women in the family had done before her. But Franklin was not swayed. Science was her intended path. Social work required nuanced people skills, and Franklin was not a "people person." She was analytical and logical and happiest solving problems with specific steps and resolutions. Also, her brothers would never have had to forsake a career for volunteer work.

Ellis finally accepted his daughter's decision. If she was going, he expected her to do well. In the months before she started at Newnham, Franklin worked in the refugee effort alongside other family members. Before her college term was to begin, she left for a vacation in France. Franklin loved the French people and language, and spent time improving her conversational French.

After returning from France, Franklin made the fifty-mile trip to Cambridge by bicycle from her home in London and settled into college life, which, by her own account, amounted to little more than another boarding school situation. There were many rules and requirements, which she shared in great detail in letters home. She had to participate in a freshman play on an evening when she had wanted to hear a lecture by a famous geneticist and chemist. She was required to eat, in evening dress, with the entire student body on occasions called the "college feast" and had to receive the principal's permission to attend an evening family gathering at a Founder's Night dinner at the Working Men's College in London.

In the beginning, Franklin probably felt like she was in over her head. Despite the modern lab facilities that had been available at St. Paul's, the science program there had poorly prepared her for Newnham. She was glad she had not stayed another year at St. Paul's, but she needed to do a great deal of catching up. After taking the final exam for her first year, she agonized that she had done poorly. Once again, her fears were exaggerated. She won first place in the exams.

She took courses in mathematics, chemistry, mineralogy, and physics and joined a mathematics society. Her specialization at Newnham was physical chemistry, a field that merges chemistry and physics to study the composition

The University of Cambridge has been a bastion of learning for men since its inception in 1209. It was 1868 before women were allowed to take exams and 1958 before they gained equal standing with male students. Newnham College was founded in 1871 as the second female college at Cambridge. (Library of Congress)

and reaction of substances as well as the structure and behavior or atoms and molecules. Franklin often worked for eight hours at a time in the Cavendish Laboratory, the home of Cambridge's Physics Department.

Franklin filled what little free time she had with walks, hockey, tennis, and ice-skating on the frozen waters of a former marshland. She took long bicycle rides, once biking fifty miles from Cambridge to London. Franklin preferred her old friends from St. Paul's to the new girls she was meeting at Newnham, who generally saw her as quiet and introverted.

While Franklin toiled away at Newnham, England prepared for war. The government built public shelters for bomb attacks and dug trenches in public parks. Individual citizens constructed their own special steel bomb shelters at home. Even Franklin's brothers and sister built an air raid shelter in the back garden of the family home. The family was especially conscious of Hitler's persecution of German Jews. Franklin was appalled at her fellow students' indifference to the anti-Semitic policies and practices of Nazi Germany. She wrote home, "Apart from your letters and *The Times*, I would still have no idea that anybody objected to Germany's treatment of the Jews. People do not talk politics here. . . ."

At the end of Franklin's first year at Cambridge, her family, including all five children, Ellis and Muriel, and the nanny, went on a summer holiday to Norway, although the threat of a German invasion loomed. Ellis worried that Jenifer would not be able to go abroad for many years once war broke out and wanted to give her the opportunity. They had a good time climbing and fishing, and were planning to cross a glacier when news reached them of the signing, on August 23, 1939, of the Nazi-Soviet Non-Aggression Pact. This put Norway clearly in either Germany's or the Soviet Union's sights. Ellis rushed the family onto a ferry and headed back to England. They made it on the second to last boat permitted to leave for England before the outbreak of World War II a little over a week later.

The Nazi-Soviet Pact between Germany and the Soviet Union promised that neither country would attack the other. Hitler did not want to repeat Germany's mistake from World War I, during which fighting on two fronts had weakened Germany's forces. He wanted to attack Poland without the Soviet Union coming to its aid. The Nazis attacked Poland on September 1. Two days later, England declared war on Germany.

As conflict raged abroad, it also did in the Franklin household. Ellis had accepted Franklin's decision to pursue science, but the war changed that. He now felt staying at the university was indulgent, especially after her brother David had left Oxford to enlist in the army. He demanded she join the Land Army, a woman's group that worked in agriculture, as her aunts had done during World War I. He also refused to pay for her second year at college.

Franklin's mother and aunt defied Ellis and promised to pay the college tuition. Franklin told her father that she planned to contribute to the war effort through her work as a scientist, where she would be much more useful than

NATIONAL SERVICE
WOMEN'S
LAND ARMY

GOD SPEED THE PLOUGH
AND THE WOMAN WHO DRIVES IT

At a time when German U-boats were cutting off supplies by sinking merchant ships off the British coastline, the women in the British Land Army kept the nation fed. By 1944 they boasted 80,000 members. (Library of Congress)

as an agricultural laborer. She reminded him that she had already helped her parents in their work for Jewish refugees, and had done volunteer work during vacations. Ellis eventually relented.

Franklin remained at the university, but was not indifferent to politics. She joined a student group raising money for refugee aid. She strongly supported the war effort and continued to write frustrated letters home about the prevailing apolitical atmosphere at Cambridge. Once, after attending a lecture on pacifism, an idea that had long been popular with students, she spent the next day trying to convince people it was immoral to stand idly by as Jews were murdered.

Franklin was concerned about the fate of European Jews and considered herself to be culturally Jewish, although she was not religious. She rejected religion and eloquently wrote in a letter home to her father in 1940:

> Science, for me, gives a partial explanation of life. In so far as it goes, it is based on fact, experience and experiment. . . . In my view, all that is necessary for faith is the belief that by doing our best we shall come nearer to success and that success in our aims (the improvement of the lot of mankind, present and future) is worth attaining. Anyone able to believe in all that religion implies obviously must have such faith, but I maintain that faith in this world is perfectly possible without faith in another world. . . . Your faith rests on the future of yourself and others as individuals, mine on the future and fate of our successors. It seems to me that yours is the more selfish. . . .

The fate of those successors hung in the balance as the war intensified. Finland, Denmark, Norway, Holland, Belgium, and France had fallen to Germany. British prime minister Neville Chamberlain, who had thought he could reach an accord with Hitler, was forced to resign and Winston Churchill became the new prime minister. The possibility loomed that Cambridge could close during the war. In that event, Franklin planned to find work as a chemist, but Ellis again objected, accusing her of being interested in nothing but science. She wrote him back in the same 1940 letter in which she had staked out her position on religion:

> You look at science (or at least talk of it) as some sort of demoralising invention of man, something apart from real life, and which must be cautiously guarded and kept separate from everyday existence. But science and everyday life cannot and should not be separated.

Cambridge opened for classes in the fall of 1940 and Franklin began her third year as the Battle of Britain—the name given to the constant bombing of London and other British population areas between September 1940 and May of 1941—began. Hitler wanted to destroy the morale of the British population by disrupting commerce and everyday life. A force of 625 German bombers was set aside for the sole purpose of attacking London. Two hundred tons of bombs were dropped daily in London, totaling more than a million bombs before the end of the war.

Though most of the bombing was concentrated on London's East Side, close to the shipping docks, bombs fell behind the Franklins' West Side home, shattering all its windows. The family realized it was time to leave London. They packed up and moved many of their belongings to an unfurnished rented house northwest of London in Hertfordshire, near Wales.

The war also changed life for Franklin at school. Many scientists left the university to take positions directly

The Blitzkrieg, or "Lightning War," decimated London with eight months of concerted but unpredictable bombing. Although 43,000 people died and more than a million homes were destroyed, the campaign failed to make the British surrender. (National Archives)

involved in war research. In a letter to her parents in October of 1940, Franklin complained that "practically the whole of the Cavendish have disappeared." The professors who remained were spread thin. In the absence of men, Cambridge even hired its first female professors in the university's seven-hundred-year history.

In 1940, during her last year at Cambridge, Franklin attended a lecture given by a French scientist named Adrienne Weill. A former pupil of chemist and Nobel laureate Marie Curie, Weill had fled France during the

Nazi occupation to teach at Newnham. She was intelligent, attractive, sophisticated, and self-assured. Franklin liked her immediately. She began to take conversational French lessons from Weill, and the two became friends. When Weill leased a house in Cambridge to rent to graduate students, Franklin helped her set it up.

As graduation neared, Franklin considered her options. Areas were opening up for women in scientific research, but she did not want to work in industry and do "science for money." She also wanted to contribute to the war effort and get her doctorate degree. Before making any decisions, she needed to take her final exams. As they neared, she grew nervous and exhausted from over-studying. When she finally took them she was overwrought and groggy from medicine she was taking for a head cold and did not complete all the questions. Franklin was certain she had destroyed any hopes for a government research grant or a student scholarship for graduate work. She did not do as well as she could have, but not as badly as she had feared. She earned a top score in her physical chemistry exam, and a second in the other part of the exam. With her supervisor's recommendation, she was offered a scholarship at Newnham and a research grant to stay another year.

Franklin began her graduate research under the physical chemist Ronald Norrish. Norrish would later win the Nobel Prize in Chemistry in 1967, but the war was a low point for him. He had lost many of his researchers to the war effort, his wife had moved away with their two daughters to a safer location, and he had started drinking heavily. The government would not give him any important war-related contracts because of his perceived instability. He was deeply unhappy and generally unpleasant to his researchers.

Norrish assigned Franklin to the study of the interactions between two compounds—formic acid and acetaldehyde (ethanol). Formic acid is a toxic, hazardous substance. Although Franklin was not thrilled with the focus of her work, which was somewhat trivial and not related to the war, she nonetheless set about her task in her usual determined manner. Norrish also put Franklin in a small, dark set of rooms, which could not have been comfortable to her, considering she was claustrophobic.

For the first time in her life, however, Franklin was living on her own, free from the constraints of home and college dorm life. She rented a room in a working class neighborhood, trying to live solely off her scholarship money. She spent her free time reading, sewing, cooking meals for friends, and listening to the radio. When her sister Jenifer was twelve years old, Rosalind invited her to stay for a few days. They traveled around Cambridge, visiting a local baker and Franklin's laboratory, where she showed her younger sister how she blew and assembled her glassware.

At age twenty-one, Franklin was independent, but also immature in many ways. Her shyness around the opposite sex bordered on the extreme. She had always abstained from dances and social events in college. When a male cousin accepted her invitation to the family's home for a weekend during Christmas holidays, Franklin paid her younger brother Roland to walk with them so they would not be alone.

In 1942, Franklin visited Adrienne Weill and made friends with several French refugees who were now living at her new boarding house. In a letter home, Franklin wrote:

> I don't know whether I meet here a particularly select French crowd but I always revel in their company. Their standard of everyday conversation is vastly superior to that of any English gathering I have been in and they are all so much more quick-witted and alive—I love listening to their language . . . though I find myself unable to take part, the pace is much too fast for me. . . . I'm thinking very seriously of moving to 12 Mill Lane—Mme Weill's place.

She made the move that summer. She delighted in the bilingual atmosphere, the energy of political debate and discussion, and the overall good feelings. Her friends in the boarding house liked her too, although they recognized her reserve. Adrienne Weill's daughter would later remember Franklin as "extremely kind, good and serious; you didn't see her smile very often."

Still, Franklin's research work was less than satisfying. Norrish had expected Franklin's experiments to yield certain results, which they failed to do because the project was flawed. Franklin wrote up her findings, detailing the problems, but Norrish refused to even look at the report, instead directing Franklin to repeat the experiments. She stood up to him and wrote to her parents about what happened:

> When I stood up to him he became most offensive
> and we had a first-class row—in fact, several. I have
> had to give in for the present but I think it is a good
> thing to have stood up to him for a time and he has
> made me despise him so completely that I shall be
> quite impervious to anything he may say to me in
> the future. He simply gave me an immense feeling
> of superiority in his presence.

With her research grant about to run out, Franklin evaluated her options for the coming year. She did not want to stay at the job at Cambridge, although Norrish, surprisingly, urged her to reapply. But if she left, she could be drafted into the military and forced into any job, such as a teacher or a factory worker. Women scientists were not necessarily drafted into scientific work; in fact, they seldom were. To give up her scholarship and doctoral work was risky.

But again luck was with her. She was offered a job at a government laboratory in southwest London called the British Coal Utilization Research Association (BCURA). The lab was in the suburbs. Franklin described it as "miles from anything, without even the consolation of a lunch-hour in town—it'll be lunch in the lab, with lab people, all horribly shut off." Nonetheless, it was war-related, scientific work under someone other than Norrish.

Working with Norrish had taken a toll on Franklin's self-confidence. Although she had always fretted about exams, she had never before questioned her ability as an experimental scientist. Now, in letters home, she expressed wistful hopes, rather than clear expectations of success in lab work. Fortunately, she was about to embark on work that would restore the confidence Norrish had eroded.

In 1942, Franklin began her job as an assistant research officer at BCURA. BCURA had been established only four years earlier and expanded rapidly with the outbreak of the war by branching into new areas of research. Its director, Dr. D. H. Bangham, sought out physicists from the universities—mostly young, eager, idealistic types, many of whom had little direct experience working with coal—who would bring fresh perspectives and knowledge of the latest technologies to help solve war-related problems.

Coal was vital to the war effort as a source of fuel, but it had other uses. Gas masks, developed in World War I to protect soldiers from chemical warfare, often used charcoal, a form of coal, as filters. Unlike gas masks with particle filters, which filter out any molecules larger than oxygen and nitrogen, or reactants, which chemically react with the toxic substances to neutralize them, charcoal gas masks simply absorb the harmful agents. The charcoal in the mask is treated with oxygen to "activate" it, opening up millions of tiny pores between the carbon atoms. This increases the surface area of the charcoal and its ability to absorb substances from gases or liquids. The chemicals bond onto the carbon surface and are safely trapped.

The chemicals used in warfare often changed and gas masks needed to be constantly modified to meet each new

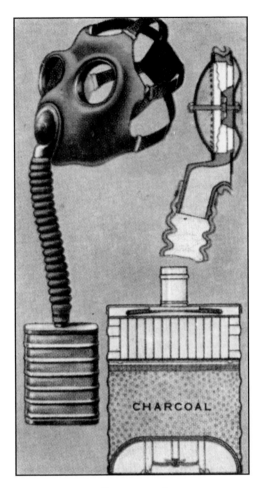

WD & HO Wills Tobacco Company issued this series of air raid precaution cigarette cards in preparation for World War II. This particular card shows the inner-workings of the Service Respirator. Franklin's work on the porosity of coal helped keep British gas masks ahead of enemy efforts. (Courtesy of the Anne Ronan Picture Library/Heritage-Images.)

threat. Franklin's task was to try to discover the reason some types of coal were more resistant to gas or water penetration than others. Franklin passed helium gas through various types of coal samples at temperatures as high as 1,000 degrees Celsius and measured their porosity.

Although Franklin later joked that she had become an expert in "holes in coal," her work at BCURA determined that varying pressure caused differences in the porosity of coal. It was an important discovery and, ironically, considering her disregard for exchanging science for money, had great industrial value.

From 1942 to 1946 Franklin performed groundbreaking work. She published five research papers bearing the results of her careful, painstaking experimentation and earned a solid scientific reputation for research on coal structures. Much of her research on the different types of coal is still used today. She also earned her PhD in 1945 based on her BCURA research.

In spite of the war, Franklin was happy in her work and personal life during this time. When she started at BCURA, she moved out of Adrienne Weill's boarding house in Cambridge into a large house in the London suburb of Putney that belonged to her uncle and aunt, but was now only occupied by her cousin Irene Franklin and a friend. There was a small garden, and a woman who came to help with the cleaning. Franklin enjoyed her independence and discovered that she liked to cook and clean for herself.

She and Irene volunteered as Air Raid Wardens, and would walk or bicycle to patrol their designated areas, inspecting to make sure people adhered to the blackout (the ban on using lights that might be visible to German bombers), getting medical help for the wounded if a bomb was dropped, and helping people to shelters during air raids. In later years, Irene would reflect fondly on those times, and on Franklin's fearlessness in walking across a dark, open common in the midst of an air raid. Yet it was Irene who, because of Franklin's claustrophobia, had to crawl into a bombed-out house one time to rescue people trapped in a cellar.

When Irene left Putney to get married and her aunt and uncle returned to their home, Franklin moved back with her parents and commuted to work. Her father was happy to have her back under the family's roof and seemed to finally accept that his eldest daughter was a working scientist.

Franklin had, perhaps because of her confidence-shaking experience with Norrish, felt vindicated by her success at BCURA and grew more self-assured. She sewed colorful pockets on her laboratory coats and, in defiance to a rule that the machine shop was off-limits to anyone but certified personnel, she would simply flip over the restrictive signs and use the machines as she pleased. Once, after accidentally thrusting a sewing needle into her knee, she walked the entire distance to the hospital alone to have it removed.

During the BCURA years, Franklin continued to go on hiking and climbing vacations. She seemed to delight in difficult, dangerous experiences. A friend of Franklin's, Anne Crawford, recalled one expedition they took together during the summer:

> One day we had made our way up Snowdon to the snow-covered Crib Goch ridge, when the mist set in. I was thankful for that as I was no longer able to see the steep drop on either side. I just managed to make my way along the ridge—driven more by my fear of Rosalind's tongue than of falling over the edge.

Another time, as Franklin hiked in the high peaks of North Wales with her friend Jean Kerslake, they met two young men who had been traveling and were staying nearby. As the sun beat down on them, they decided to go for a swim in the nearby lake. None of them had bathing suits, so they swam without any clothes.

As the war drew near a close, Franklin became bored with BCURA and was ready for a change. She briefly considered going back to Cambridge to work for Norrish again, but she could not bring herself to do it. "He's merely expressed willingness to have me work for him for a year as an unpaid stooge . . . and he is stupid, bigoted, deceitful, ill-mannered and tyrannical," she wrote to her parents. Writing to Adrienne Weill, who had returned to Paris after it was liberated from the Nazis, Franklin assumed a humorous tone, but her message was clear:

> In spite of persistent efforts to move, I am still at [B]CURA, which is still in its usual state of crisis. I am free to leave as soon as I can find another job. If ever you hear of anybody anxious for the services of a physical chemist who knows very little physical chemistry, but quite a lot about the holes in coal, please let me know.

When the war in Europe ended in May of 1945, Franklin was still casting about, looking for her next opportunity. With a PhD in physical chemistry, and scientific publications on the way, her future was hopeful, but presently unfocused.

That summer, when travel restrictions were lifted, Franklin set off for a climbing adventure in the French Alps with

Franklin, in June of 1946. She was admired by those not threatened by her assertiveness. (Courtesy of the National Portrait Gallery, London.)

her friend Jean. They stayed in youth hostels and visited Weill on the way to the mountains. Franklin enjoyed the rigorous itinerary. They stayed in cheap hotels, slept on hard floors in hostels, used outhouses, and crossed makeshift bridges that had been destroyed and hastily rebuilt during the war. Once, they climbed to the peak of a steep mountain using ice picks and ropes, only to discover when they returned much later than they had anticipated that a search party was being formed to look for them. Back in England, Franklin wrote to her mother, "I am quite sure I could wander happily in France for ever. I love the people, the country and the food."

In the fall of 1946, Franklin presented a paper on her coal research at a conference at the Royal Institution in London. Following her own presentation, she pointed out errors in another speaker's calculations. She was forceful and self-assured, and drew the positive attention of Marcel Mathieu and Jacques Mering, two French scientists in attendance who were also friends of Weill's. Mathieu held an important position in a French governmental agency that funded a large part of the scientific research conducted in France.

Weill made sure that Mathieu and Franklin were introduced, and they took to each other almost immediately. They would remain lifelong friends. But it was Jacques Mering who caught her eye. Mering was intelligent, charismatic, and rakishly handsome. Franklin apparently became infatuated with him. Unfortunately, Mering had both a wife and mistress back home.

Franklin's proficiency in French assured Mathieu that she would be able to work in France. She charmed him, and within a month he offered her a job as a physical chemist working on coal research in a Paris laboratory. She enthusiastically accepted. Franklin was about to embark on the happiest years of her life.

three
LIFE IN PARIS

Franklin moved to Paris in February of 1947 to begin her job with the Central State Chemistry Laboratories (Laboratoire des Services Chimiques de l'Etat). It was in Paris that she would master the techniques of X-ray crystallography that she later applied to DNA. Her teacher was Jacques Mering, the man she had met, and been attracted to, in London.

In France, Franklin worked in a government laboratory conducting pure research without any industrial objective. It was her dream job. Fourteen other researchers worked on staff, with six technicians, all under Jacques Mering's supervision. Franklin impressed Mering and the other researchers with her outstanding experimental skills and strong temperament.

Culturally and politically, Paris was a world apart from

Paris, after its liberation from the Nazis in 1944, boasted a vibrant and active intellectual community. The heady atmosphere of freedom suited Franklin. She practiced her profession without the gender politics that dominated her field in Britain. (Library of Congress)

London. Equal pay for equal work for men and women was the law. Women could pursue professional careers without conflict or suspicion from their male colleagues. Most men seemed to truly respect intelligent women and to enjoy their companionship. Conversation was fast-paced and emotional. Rosalind flourished in the lively debates held after work in the cafés. She loved the French language, writing to her parents, "I've been told several times my French is best when I'm angry. I had a glorious row this a.m. in a shoe store that sold me a pair of straps of wildly different length. I enjoyed it immensely."

Weill helped Franklin find an inexpensive room near the Left Bank of the Seine River. Rosalind got along well with her landlady, a widow, and adored her top-floor bedroom, which had been converted from a library. She was given strict rules to follow—the house must be quiet after 9:30 PM, she had kitchen privileges only after the landlady had finished her own supper, and she was allowed use of the room with the bathtub once a week. The rest of the week she was to wash using a basin behind a screen. None of those rules bothered Franklin; they appealed to her spartan side. Franklin's salary was modest, but her rent was one-third what she would pay elsewhere and she could walk or bicycle to work along the Seine in thirty minutes, or take the bus.

Her parents were less excited with her new living arrangements. They did not want their daughter living like a commoner. Franklin responded to their concerns:

> Of course my standard of living is lower than at home. . . . Of course I appreciate conventional comforts and of course I would rather the food situation here were normal. . . . but provided one does not go below a certain minimum none of these things are of supreme importance to me. . . . I find life interesting. . . . I have good friends though my circle is naturally smaller than in London but I find infinite kindness and goodwill among the people I work with. All this is far more important than a large meat ration or more frequent baths.

Franklin's laboratory was in an old, charming building that had not been originally intended to house a research facility. The large, airy, informal rooms suited the people who worked there. Franklin's colleagues were young and sociable. They took a real interest in each other's lives, and freely discussed almost every imaginable topic. They lunched together in local restaurants and brewed coffee in a laboratory beaker. Sometimes they went dancing in the evenings or hosted dinner parties. In the summer

Vittorio Luzzati snapped this candid photo of Franklin. Her close friendship with Luzzati and his wife endured throughout Franklin's life. (Courtesy of the National Portrait Gallery, London.)

they swam in a nearby pool and took weekend trips to the country or hiked in the mountains. Franklin became especially good friends with two couples, Vittorio and Denise Luzzati, and David and Anne Sayre. Vittorio and David both worked in the lab.

Franklin became more stylish in Paris and began to wear more feminine fashions. Her friends and family in London noticed the change. Some of them thought she might even be in love. "Something *happened* to Ros in Paris," her cousin Ursula later commented. However, one could only speculate. Franklin always kept her deepest personal feelings to herself.

Franklin's professional life during the four years she spent in Paris was as fruitful as her personal life. X-ray crystallography, sometimes called X-ray diffraction, was a relatively new technique and Franklin was initially unfamiliar with it. X-rays, which make it possible to see inside non-transparent objects, were first discovered in 1895 by Wilhelm Conrad Roentgen. Other scientists, including Sir Lawrence Bragg, followed up on Roentgen's work, and looked for the practical applications of X-rays.

All matter is made up of molecules, which are two or more atoms chemically bonded together. A water molecule, for example, is made up of three atoms—two atoms of hydrogen and one of oxygen. If the atoms were to be separated, the substance would cease to be water. Atoms are too small to see under microscopes, but when X-rays are shot at atomic structures of matter in its crystalline form, the X-rays diffract, or bounce off, onto the film. When that pattern is analyzed, it is possible to discover the form and structure of the molecules. From there, scientists can deduce any number of things about its function and behavior.

In 1912 it was discovered that X-rays, like all light, could be diffracted. When a beam of X-rays was passed through a crystal onto a photographic plate, the plate could be developed and the pattern could be studied. Scientists could then mathematically work out how the atoms were arranged in the crystal. The patterns would differ from substance to substance, depending on the atomic structure.

Franklin soon became an expert in X-ray crystallography techniques, which she used to explore the molecular structure of a number of carbon-based substances. She worked with carbons whose diffraction patterns were often foggy and complicated, and required extensive mathematical analysis to interpret. In Franklin's day, prior to computers, these calculations were painstakingly done by hand.

Franklin had a gift for this type of experimental work. Many other scientists would view such tasks as a necessary but unpleasant part of the job, but she enjoyed the process of experimentation. She also had a knack for recognizing the similarities between seemingly dissimilar materials. She was the first scientist to recognize that coals, as well as other organic chemicals, including plastics, have common characteristics, and was able to divide coals, plastics and some other solid organic substances into two groups.

Although synthetic graphite had been produced for years, Franklin was one of the first to research what happens when carbon is turned into graphite. By using temperatures up to 3,000 degrees Celsius, she discovered that some carbons could be converted into graphite through high temperatures, and others could not. These two types of carbons had different physical properties—the graphitizing carbons were soft and nonporous, while the non-graphitizing carbons were hard, with low density.

Again, there were industrial uses for Franklin's discoveries. Non-graphitizing carbons—now called "vitreous" or "glassy" carbon—could be made into solid shapes that resisted high temperatures and corrosion, which make them excellent heat and electrical conductors.

Her work was not without danger though, and it is unclear how seriously Franklin took the threat of working around X-rays. Although a blood disease associated with radiation poisoning caused the death of Marie Curie in 1934, the ill effects of X-ray exposure were still not well understood. Tolerance dosage guidelines for radiation were established but changed frequently, depending on the scientific knowledge of the day. What was permissible was not necessarily what was safe. Franklin was regularly exposed to radiation when she positioned the samples. The camera could only be focused when the beam was on, and she took few or no precautions as she moved about in the beam. None of the staff at the lab,

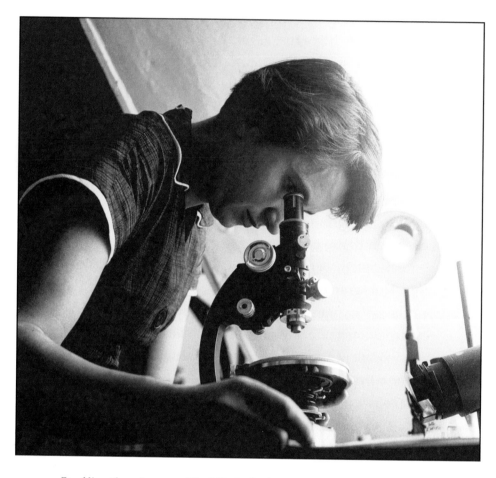

Franklin, at her microscope. The skills she developed in Paris became the foundation of her future success. (© Museum of London)

including Franklin, seemed particularly concerned over the dangers of radiation, or went out of their way to wear the lead apron that was available for protection.

Franklin published seven scientific papers during her time in Paris. She learned a great deal from Jacques

Mering. He later admitted he was very much taken with Franklin's intelligence and beauty. She clearly was intrigued with him as well. They spent much time together, evenings as well as days, working in the lab.

As Franklin's professional reputation grew, she was asked to speak at scientific conferences. She participated as both a speaker and a commenting member of the audience. In a short time, she became one of the world's leading X-ray diffraction specialists.

Upon the end of the war in 1945, scientists who had previously been focused on war-related problems were free to explore new avenues of research. Scientists who had spent most of their lives in one field of endeavor and had gained acclaim for their work began to think of fields that were far away from their earlier work.

Erwin Schrodinger, who won the Nobel Prize in Physics in 1933, left Berlin that year to protest the persecution of the Jews. After working at prestigious universities throughout Europe, he wound up in Ireland, at the Dublin Institute of Advanced Studies in 1940. In Dublin, Schrodinger began a series of lectures that excited widespread interest from other scientists as well as the general public. He proposed the radical idea that physics, chemistry, and biology should be a combined science. Since living organisms were made of molecules, atoms, and chemical substances, why, he asked, was biology treated as separate from chemistry and physics? After all, living and nonliving substances follow the same scientific principles.

A book composed of his lectures was published in 1941 entitled *What Is Life?* The book generated great excitement among physicists, who clamored at the idea of a whole new biological realm to ponder and solve with the principles of physics. The new field of biophysics was born, altering the focus of many researchers, including Franklin.

Although she loved working in Paris, Franklin knew she would eventually have to return to London. She was a foreigner working for the French government, and it was unlikely she could stay on a permanent, secure basis. She began to search in earnest for a job in Britain. She applied to Birkbeck College, where the eminent crystallographer J. D. Bernal had recently joined the staff, but she did not get the position. She also considered the Royal Institution, but was so put off by her prospective supervisor that she ruled it out.

Franklin realized she would have better opportunities after more of her papers were published. When her ninth paper, "The Interpretation of Diffuse X-ray Diagrams of Carbon," was published in the scientific journal *Acta Crystallographic*, she was disappointed that Jacques Mering refused to have his name published as co-author, although the work was a joint effort. Mering was angry that Franklin was planning to return to London.

When another paper was accepted for publication in the highly respected scientific journal *Nature,* Franklin realized the timing was right to return to London. Still, she had mixed feelings about leaving Paris. Her life there was satisfying, she had made good friends, and her work was going well. But her best career prospects were on the other side of the channel.

In the spring of 1950, Franklin applied for a research fellowship at King's College, London. King's biophysics unit was headed by the energetic and charismatic John Randall, who had been successful in his research career in industry at the General Electric Company. Randall recognized the importance of encouraging links between the branches of biology. He courted a special interest in biophysics and, because of his reputation, was able to secure large amounts of research money for the new field. He was also made director of the Biophysics Research Unit by the MRC (the Medical Research Council), which was the main British agency funding biology research related to medicine. When he arrived from General Electric, he brought loads of scientific apparatus, including luminescent material, spectroscopes, and X-ray diffraction equipment.

Randall had a knack for gathering bright scientists around him, and encouraging creativity and competition among them. After an interview, Franklin was awarded a three-year fellowship to begin at King's in the autumn of 1950, working under the direction of Professor Randall. Her research at King's was to apply X-ray diffraction methods to the heating and dehydrating of proteins. It would be her first professional opportunity to study biological, or living, organisms. Still unsure about her decision to leave Paris, she requested a one-year's postponement. She was to begin at King's in the fall of 1951.

four

FRICTION AND
DIFFRACTION

Heredity—the passing down of features and characteristics from parents to their children and subsequent descendants—has long been recognized as observable fact. Why some children more closely resemble their parents or one parent more than the other, or why some characteristics seem to skip a generation, was less understood. Somehow, traits were inherited, but how or why this happened largely remained a mystery.

In 1865, Gregor Mendel, an Austrian monk, conducted a series of painstaking experiments with garden peas and discovered that specific characteristics travel by inheritance units—later known as genes—that can be mathematically calculated and predicted. His discovery went unrecognized for years, until other scientists stumbled across his findings and began to build on them.

Genes actually carry the recipes for making different proteins. Proteins are sequences of amino acids strung together in different patterns. Each protein performs a specific task. Proteins are the life and labor forces of our bodies. Their job is to orchestrate the cell's structure and function; they are responsible for all of the body's systems, as well as the communication and transportation of chemicals—usually other proteins—between cells. The process of making proteins is called protein synthesis.

In 1871, Friedrich Miescher found that chromosomes, X-shaped bodies found in the nucleus of each cell, are composed of deoxyribonucleic acid (DNA) and protein. At the time, no one knew the function or significance of chromosomes. Then, in 1910, Thomas Hunt Morgan discovered that they carry the genetic information for the cell. If the gene was in the chromosome, and if the chromosome was made of protein and DNA, which substance was the gene made of—protein or DNA?

Little was known about the molecular structure of either protein or DNA. X-ray diffraction techniques offered a promising approach to learn more. The problem was that as the size of the molecule increased, the diffraction patterns they produced were so complex that they often defied mathematical analysis in the pre-computer era.

But biological research was progressing rapidly. Before the war, biologists were able to get X-ray diffraction patterns of DNA fibers, which were then thought to mainly function as a binding agent for the more complex protein in the cell. After the war, microbiologist Oswald

Avery, revisiting experiments done in 1928 by an English physician, made a remarkable breakthrough. Using pneumonia-causing bacteria, he discovered that when he took DNA from a dead strain of bacteria and put it in a living strain, the hereditary characteristics from the original were given to the host. Avery had answered the question left after Morgan's discovery. DNA—not protein—is the carrier of the genetic code.

This discovery, of course, raised a whole new series of puzzling questions. Each protein molecule is made up of amino acids linked together in long chains, with twenty possible combinations of amino acids making up each link. That was why it had seemed most plausible that proteins contained the complex genetic information that directed the cell. DNA, on the other hand, is made up of only a few relatively simple chemicals. It did not seem possible that these few chemicals—repeating units called nucleotides—could carry the copious amount of information that would guide protein synthesis. But Avery had proven that DNA did just that. How was it possible?

This question of the structure and mechanics of DNA loomed over postwar science in much the same way questions about electromagnetism and the structure of light had preoccupied researchers at the beginning of the century. The opportunity for Franklin to use her skills with X-ray diffraction on the most highly sought-after scientific mystery of the era was exciting and provocative. It was certainly a challenge. Prior efforts at using crystallography to find DNA's structure had yielded poor images and little data. Even if she were able to find the structure, there was no guarantee that the discovery would reveal how DNA regulated a cell's biochemistry or replicated and passed on the genetic code. But Franklin was excited by the possibility that it might and was eager to get started.

Unable to initially find an apartment, she temporarily moved back in with her parents. She was at least spared the indignity of reoccupying her childhood room because Ellis and Muriel had sold their larger home a while back. Franklin must have felt totally deflated; she had been an independent, respected, stylish Paris scientist, but now was reduced to living with her parents again.

Even though Paris had been occupied by the Nazis during the war, it had not been bombed like London had been in 1940 and 1941. The whole city showed battle scars and was riddled with scores of craters and bombsites dotting the landscape. Buildings leaned dangerously on cracked foundations and houses were obscured behind wooden scaffoldings. Food was still rationed. It would take years before a sense of normalcy began to return to London.

At King's College, Franklin's new workplace, a bomb had gouged the main courtyard, leaving a hole seven feet deep and fifty-eight feet long. The biophysics department was located around the bomb crater. Excavation was proceeding while she was there for the construction of the new physics building. Rubble was piled everywhere. The dingy, basement laboratory she was to work in stood in stark

The main building at King's College. (King's College, London)

contrast to the airy rooms she had occupied in Paris.

She also resented the English gender bias that had seemed so absent in France. Many women scientists worked at King's, but they were not permitted to enter the men's Senior Common Room or eat in the men's considerably fancier dining facility.

As Franklin tried to come to terms with all of the disappointing realities of her life in London, she bemoaned the "vacant stupid faces and child-like complacency" of her English compatriots. The person who showed her around the labs later remembered how resistant she was to meeting people, and how tightly wound she seemed. Others in the lab thought she acted snobbish and very class-conscious.

Franklin had originally been hired to examine proteins in solutions, but Professor Randall now wrote to tell her she had been switched to DNA research. Franklin welcomed the change. She considered DNA a much more exciting subject. Randall's letter also outlined Franklin's role in the research, informing her that two others who had been involved in DNA X-ray work—Maurice Wilkins and Alec Stokes—were being moved to other tasks, leaving Franklin in charge of the X-ray crystallography effort at King's.

Maurice Wilkins, the assistant director of the Medical Research Council (MRC), had been involved with DNA research at King's for several years. He was the primary person directly involved in X-ray work. In fact, it had been Wilkins who had convinced Professor Randall to switch Franklin to DNA research. Along with his graduate student, Raymond Gosling, Wilkins had been getting excellent results. But Randall's letter to Franklin barely mentioned Wilkins, except in reference to Gosling, who would now work for her.

Randall had apparently omitted Wilkins's active participation in DNA research deliberately. Randall had long been fascinated with the structure of DNA and, after spending so much energy and time building up his laboratory, now wanted to be closer to actual DNA research.

During the war, Maurice Wilkins worked on the Manhattan Project to build the atomic bombs that were eventually dropped on Hiroshima and Nagasaki. Wilkins's horror at his own involvement in the bombing of population centers led him to DNA research after the war. (Courtesy of Getty Images.)

But Wilkins, who had considerable sway within the MRC, was unlikely to give it up on his own. Randall planned to maneuver Wilkins away from DNA entirely and to have Franklin report directly to him. This way Randall would have more of a hand in her research.

Randall called a meeting in January of 1951 to introduce Franklin to some of her new colleagues and to discuss the direction of their work. Franklin met her new assistant, Raymond Gosling, the doctoral student previously working for Maurice Wilkins. Gosling was from the University College Medical School, and was very happy to be at King's. With his easygoing personality, he joked that he was "the PhD slave boy handed over in chains" from Wilkins to Franklin. Raymond described Rosalind as "not tall but of reasonable height and striking looks. She had wonderfully lustrous dark eyes. I found her very attractive as did I think everyone who worked with her. She was at that time about 30/31 and I was only 23/24, so I was somewhat in awe of her because she had a very strong personality and she was an assured scientist."

As Franklin began to settle in, she found, to her dismay, that a group of former military men had temporarily joined the biophysics unit in order to complete their undergraduate degrees and was staying on to work as a team. Their gruff, barroom antics and tough-talking manners grated on Franklin's more cosmopolitan sensibilities, reinforcing her sense of isolation.

Franklin had to finish writing up the coal research she had done in Paris before she could begin working on DNA. She and Wilkins did not have much contact at the King's lab to discuss their common DNA interests for a while. They did find themselves together at the fairly empty lab on Saturdays and ate lunch together several times. When Wilkins and Franklin spent time outside of the lab, they talked about topics often unrelated to science: politics, books, theater, and other subjects of mutual interest.

Wilkins later mused that their backgrounds were similar in so many ways, and, being close in age, they should have been able to forge a friendship. Both had attended Cambridge, and their families shared similar interests in education and social justice. His family, even more so than Franklin's, was dedicated to higher education for women. Their fathers both supported the Working Men's College. Franklin and Wilkins even shared similar views on politics.

Yet their personalities clashed, intensely and almost immediately. Franklin respected men who were powerful and assertive, like her father, and whom she could learn from, like Jacques Mering. She enjoyed debate and the challenge of defending her intellectual positions. Her arguments were passionate and challenging, as was her personality. Wilkins, by contrast, was vulnerable, timid, and mild-mannered. He was averse to conflict and spirited debate, and would withdraw in silence when challenged.

Franklin was shy, as close friends knew, but she hid her shyness with assertiveness. She did not tolerate weakness, either in herself or in others. It is possible that she simply wrote off Wilkins as weak and foolish early in their relationship. Their first professional interaction would set the stage for what was to follow, and it would never improve, only intensify.

Wilkins had been attempting to hydrate DNA fibers in order to examine their changing characteristics, but the

DNA fiber was not absorbing the water easily. Franklin quickly solved the problem because she knew a salt solution would best enable the hydrogen gas used inside the camera to keep the air moist around the fibers. Wilkins had been hesitant to use salt, fearing it would affect the DNA, but he readily admitted she had been right. From Franklin's perspective, the hydration solution was a well-known method that Wilkins should have known, and she told him so. Wilkins detected a superior attitude from Franklin. He surmised that she was a difficult, overbearing woman.

Raymond Gosling, who liked both Wilkins and Rosalind, was a student with little power to mediate their personality conflict, although he did make an effort. When Wilkins asked for suggestions on how to improve his relationship with Franklin, Gosling told him to bring her chocolates. Wilkins did as Gosling suggested, but Franklin remained frosty.

Further complicating the situation, Wilkins had apparently been led to believe that Franklin would be serving as his assistant. He had no idea how respected she was from her work in Paris, nor of what Randall had communicated to Franklin in his letter and at the meeting. Franklin, however, was clear on what Randall had told her. She was to build an X-ray crystallography unit and carry out or supervise all DNA X-ray work at King's. As soon as she finished her coal papers, she set out to do exactly that.

Before Franklin's arrival at King's, Wilkins and Gosling had gone to another laboratory at Birkbeck College, hoping to buy a new, recently invented apparatus that focused X-ray beams more finely. To their delight, one of the inventors, Werner Ehrenberg, had given them the original model. One of Franklin's first projects was to assemble the apparatus and to make any necessary adjustments. She set about rebuilding the Ehrenberg prototype, assisted by Gosling. They designed a microcamera that would attach to the new equipment and tilt for better focusing. It took them almost eight months to assemble the apparatus. Once completed, they began to focus on a set of excellent DNA fibers given to King's by Professor Rudolph Signer at a conference in Berne, Switzerland.

Franklin used this camera while at King's. Her patience and precision were well suited to the tedious process of taking diffraction images. (King's College, London)

In the meantime, Randall had asked Wilkins to speak on large molecules at a conference in Naples, Italy. Wilkins explained to the audience of international scientists why King's was concentrating on nucleic acid and showed them the sharpest image of a DNA molecule that any of the scientists in attendance had ever seen.

In the audience was twenty-three-year-old Dr. James Watson, a brilliant American zoologist who, after reading Schrodinger's *What Is Life?* in college, had immediately decided to dedicate himself to genetics. He had come to the Naples conference specifically to hear the lecture on DNA and was thrilled to learn that not only could DNA be crystallized, it could also be analyzed from diffraction photographs. Watson hoped to somehow join Wilkins in working on DNA and looked unsuccessfully for an opportunity over the next several days to make inroads with him socially. "I proceeded to forget Wilkins, but not his DNA photograph," said Watson. "A potential key to the secret of life was impossible to push out of my mind. The fact that I was unable to interpret it did not bother me. It was certainly better to imagine myself becoming famous than maturing into a stifled academic who had never risked a thought."

In July, Wilkins spoke at another conference at the Cavendish Laboratory, Cambridge University's Department of Physics. By then, he had compared the Signer DNA pattern with DNA samples from herrings, humans, calves and sepia sperm, and found them to be basically the same. Protein was structurally different in different

Wilkins presenting several X-ray diffraction photos of DNA. (Courtesy of Getty Images.)

species. But if DNA was the same, it would be biologically important, and easier to map. Although he did not get very good fibers or patterns from these other DNA samples, they all seemed to show a central X pattern, a strong indication of a helix shape.

Wilkins's presentation drew applause, and he reveled in his favorable reception. As usual he felt a bit awkward, but was satisfied when he overheard Max Perutz, the witty and distinguished molecular biologist studying protein structure at the Cavendish lab, comment on how interesting his lecture had been. Wilkins was therefore caught off guard, and visibly shaken, when Franklin approached him after his speech to attack him for continuing with his X-ray work. "Go back to your microscopes!" she instructed him.

Wilkins was baffled. His presentation had shown good progress in his research. "Why should she want me to stop?" he later wrote. "What right had she to tell me what I should do?" He probably wondered if it had been the success of his talk that had disturbed her. Maybe if he did not respond or make an issue of it, things would return to normal.

Things did not return to normal, of course. According to what Franklin had been told by Randall, Wilkins was not supposed to be doing X-ray work anymore. Yet there he was, unwarrantedly reporting on research results that Franklin thought she was in charge of. If the two had been able to sit down and hash it out, perhaps the misunderstandings, and Randall's duplicity, would have come to light. It never happened.

In September, after returning from a conference in the United States, Wilkins, in spite of his earlier experience, was excited to tell Franklin what he had learned. He had met Erwin Chargaff, a biochemist from Columbia University in New York, who had been very interested in their DNA research. Chargaff had been happy to share what he had recently discovered about the nitrogen bases in DNA. Most scientists working with DNA knew by that time that it was composed of a string of nucleotides, each of which contained a sugar (deoxyribose), a phosphate, and one of the four nitrogen bases—adenine (A), thymine (T), guanine (G), and cytosine (C). Chargaff had discovered that, of the four bases, adenine always appears in the same amount as thymine in DNA. Similarly, guanine is present in equal amounts to cytosine. Scientists had previously thought that all four bases were in parity. It was a critical discovery, but neither Chargaff nor Wilkins fully recognized its implications at the time.

When Wilkins tried to report Chargoff's findings to Franklin, she interrupted to tell him about new results she had found while he was gone. After perfecting a method to stabilize the humidity inside the camera, she had been able to take diffraction photographs of the Signer DNA in both its wet and dry states. From there, she had isolated an "A" and a "B" form of DNA. The A form was dry, compact, and crystalline, and yielded a busy, complicated diffraction pattern. The B, or humidified form, showed a simpler pattern that better lent itself to analysis. Prior attempts at photographing DNA did not reveal much information; now it was clear why. The wet and the dry form of DNA looked very different from each other, and earlier photographs had blurred combinations of the two forms. Franklin also found that Wilkins and Gosling had erred in their earlier research. The samples were not as wet as they had thought. Wilkins "felt frustrated not only because Raymond and I had been mistaken about the humidity of A-DNA, but also because Rosalind's step forward deserved praise, and it was not easy to

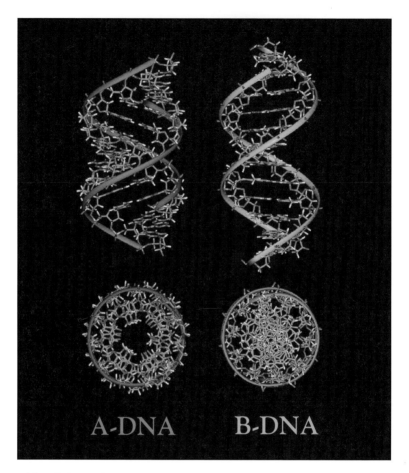

A-DNA   B-DNA

Although the two forms arise simply from the strand of DNA being wet or dry, the structure of the forms looked quite different to early researchers. The more compact A form that was Franklin's project presented a far greater challenge.

give that praise when she seemed to be pleased by our mistake."

Franklin's early photographs of the B form showed signs of a helical structure. The A form was more complicated and difficult to work with. Without water, the DNA fibers coiled and crystallized, and when she increased the humidity they would lengthen back into the B form.

Franklin deduced that the phosphate groups (a known component of DNA that tend to soak up water) must be on the outside, because of the ease with which the molecule seemed to absorb water when exposed to it.

Franklin presented her findings at a seminar in November 1951 at King's. James Watson was in the audience. Since his failed attempt to befriend Wilkins in Naples, he had managed to find a position with Max Perutz at the Cavendish and had asked Wilkins if he could attend Franklin's lecture.

Both the Cavendish and King's were funded by the same source, the MRC, which was not likely to fund duplicate projects. Watson later admitted that, "At this time molecular work on DNA in England, was, for all practical purposes, the personal property of Maurice Wilkins . . . at King's College." Watson bided his time, working at the Cavendish on the three-dimensional structures of proteins. Knowing very little about X-ray diffraction, Watson did not learn much from Franklin's presentation. He took no notes and remembered little of what she said.

He did, however, get another opportunity at meeting Wilkins and this time he was more successful. They went out to dinner together. "To my surprise" Watson wrote, "Maurice seemed buoyed up by my presence. The aloofness that existed when we first met in Naples had vanished." Wilkins was pleased to find someone who took such interest in DNA. The friendship that was forged that evening would prove historical.

five

PHOTO 51

The researchers at King's and the Cavendish Laboratory were not the only ones interested in discovering the structure of DNA. Linus Pauling, a famous chemist at the California Institute of Technology (Cal Tech), had also taken up the challenge. In addition to being a chemist, Pauling was a humanitarian and political activist who would eventually win a Nobel Peace Prize in addition to a Nobel Prize in Chemistry. In 1951, he had discovered the alpha helix—the most important regular structure in proteins—and had pioneered the use of models as a method to suggest possible structures for complex biological molecules. He now set his sights on DNA. But his efforts to get a look at the research of English scientists were repeatedly thwarted. He traveled to England and contacted Randall to ask for copies of DNA X-ray

Because of his involvement in an anti-nuclear weapon group chaired by Albert Einstein, Linus Pauling was barred several times from leaving the country by the U.S. government. In the end, Pauling was granted a passport just in time to accept his Nobel Prize in 1954. (Courtesy of Tom Hollyman / Photo Researchers, Inc.)

photographs taken at King's. Randall rebuffed him, saying, "It would not be fair to [Wilkins and his team] or to the efforts of the laboratory as a whole, to hand these over to you," he wrote.

Randall did remind Pauling that Wilkins would soon present a summary of the DNA work being done at King's at a conference in the United States. Pauling could learn more at that time. Wilkins had asked Stokes if he could figure out whether King's most recent X-ray photographs showed a helical structure. Stokes took twenty-four hours and mathematically determined that, yes, it would be a helix.

After presenting his findings in the U.S., Wilkins returned to King's lab to learn that Franklin had taken some remarkable photos of the two forms of DNA. Her careful, painstaking preparation of the DNA fibers through chemical hydration had produced what crystallographer J. D. Bernal later described as "among the most beautiful X-ray photographs of any substance ever taken." Excited by Franklin's incredibly clear B-pattern photo, Wilkins suggested that they collaborate to find out if DNA samples that Chargaff had given him at the U.S. conference would also form a B pattern. Franklin blew up at Wilkins. What gall he had to try to push his way into her work, done mostly in isolation, but now suddenly worthy of his collaboration. From Franklin's perspective, Wilkins was not even supposed to be involved with DNA diffraction work.

Randall had known about the hostility between Wilkins and Franklin. He had initially tried to ignore it, but now had no choice but to try to smooth things out. He called Franklin and Wilkins into his office. After talking, they agreed that from then on, Franklin would take her new X-ray diffraction camera and the Signer DNA and concentrate on the A form, and Wilkins would research the B form with his old camera and the DNA samples Chargaff had given him. That way, they would not need to interact or communicate.

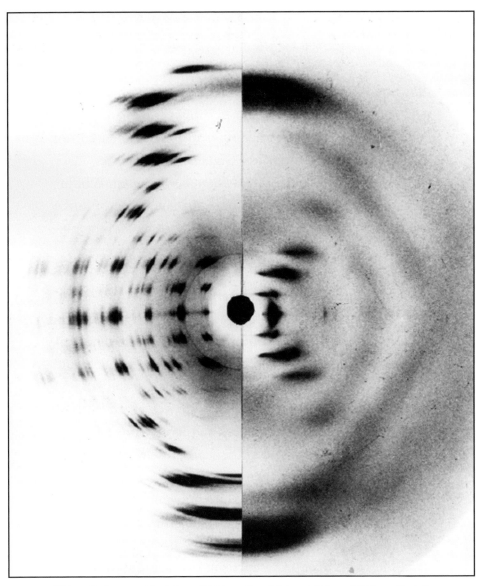

This split image with A-form DNA on the right and B-form DNA on the left illustrates how much more complex Franklin's project was. Despite her superior equipment, images of the B-form always appeared fuzzy. (King's College, London)

Although taking the Chargaff DNA was Wilkins's idea, he soon regretted it. The Chargaff samples were of poor quality next to Signer's. He was unable to crystallize them or hydrate them into the A and B forms. No one knew quite how Signer had managed to prepare his excellent samples, and efforts at the King's lab to replicate them were not successful. After their fractious split, Wilkins dared not ask Franklin for some of the Signer DNA back.

While Franklin busily went about her research, Wilkins languished with poor fibers and old equipment. Unlike Franklin, he did not work well without input and interaction. Working at King's became more and more problematic for Wilkins. He began visiting the Cavendish Laboratory where an old friend, physicist Francis Crick, had taught himself crystallography and was working on his PhD on X-ray diffraction of proteins. Crick was charming, positive, and outgoing. Wilkins took comfort in the lively and stimulating atmosphere surrounding Crick at the lab and at his home. Crick's French wife Odile welcomed Wilkins and served up delicious dinners and lively conversation.

James Watson had also befriended Crick when they met at the Cavendish lab, where both were studying crystallography and plant viruses. Their knowledge and interests were complementary and their personalities meshed. Both delighted in their conversations at the lab and at the local pub, the Eagle. They shared a sort of youthful arrogance, as well as a common interest in DNA, and were eager to be the first to uncover its structure. Sparked by Linus Pauling's success in using model building to reveal the alpha helix in proteins, Watson prodded Crick to build a model using Wilkins's theory of the helical structure for DNA.

Model building was not a new method in science, but

many scientists were revisiting it in light of Pauling's accomplishment. The approach combined three elements: theoretical understanding of chemistry (particularly chemical bonds), X-ray diffraction, and model building. Pauling showed that when used as one part of this triad approach, models could visually demonstrate a complex structural form. The pieces of the model would represent different chemical components, and their structures would correspond to each component's bonding properties. This allowed scientists to piece together the structure of a molecule like a giant, three-dimensional puzzle. James Watson was a strong proponent of this method. He later wrote:

> Pauling's accomplishment was a product of common sense, not the result of complicated mathematical reasoning. Equations occasionally crept into his argument, but in most cases words would have sufficed. The key to Linus' success was his reliance on the simple laws of structural chemistry. The a-helix had not been found by only staring at X-ray pictures; the essential trick, instead, was to ask which atoms like to sit next to each other. In place of pencil and paper, the main working tools were a set of molecular models superficially resembling the toys of preschool children. We could thus see no reason why we should not solve DNA in the same way.

Although Franklin was not against model building, she thought that, without factual support, all the models in the world would never prove anything. She depended on gathering hard, empirically observed facts and carefully documented data. Model building might be an appropriate strategy, but only after piecing together enough information on which to base one. The model would support the facts, and the facts would prove the model. Building a speculative model in the hope that the data might happen to support it seemed to be a waste of time.

Watson continued to push Crick to help him build a DNA model. But Crick's charge was to finish his thesis on proteins, not to divert his efforts to DNA. Besides, DNA work belonged to King's, and it was generally understood that one lab would not actively try to "scoop" another.

The Cavendish Laboratory is the home of Cambridge University's physics department. (Washington University, St. Louis)

Early in November, Bruce Fraser, a member of a group connected to the biophysics unit at King's, asked Franklin for her input on a DNA model he was building as part of his doctoral thesis. His model represented a synthesis of the thinking of many scientists in the field. It was centered around a triple helix, with the phosphate bonds on the outside, as had been advocated by Franklin. Franklin's comment about Fraser's model sums up her thinking about the use of models: "That's very nice—how are you going to prove it is the solution?"

Around that same time, Crick invited Wilkins to come for a weekend visit to his home in Cambridge. James Watson was also visiting. Wilkins caught them up with the DNA work at King's. He repeated what he had presented at the seminar in July, which rekindled the bad feelings of the saga with Franklin and the dressing down he had received for what she perceived as an infingement on her area of research. Watson and Crick sympathized with Wilkins for having to put up with Franklin, who Wilkins complained had virtually locked him out of DNA research by taking his best samples and camera.

Wilkins, thrilled to find someone interested in his research, talked freely about what was going on at King's. He had no reason to believe he should be more circumspect. No one at the Cavendish lab was working on DNA, at least not officially. Watson and Crick both urged Wilkins to build a model but Wilkins had already spent his model making passion by collaborating with Fraser. He did not follow up on their suggestion.

A week after the November seminar at King's where Franklin presented her findings of the A and B forms of DNA, James Watson and Francis Crick built their own model of DNA. They based it on their hours of discussion, Watson's memory of what Franklin had presented at King's and their memory of what Wilkins had told them.

Crick telephoned Wilkins to inform him that he and Watson had built the model, and invited him to Cambridge to see it. Wilkins gathered Franklin, Gosling, Bruce Fraser, and another colleague, Bill Seeds, and they took a train to Cambridge to see what Watson and Crick were up to. At the Cavendish lab, the group saw a model of a three-chain helix with the nitrogen bases flopping around on the outside of the helix, and the phosphates held together along the inside axis.

Franklin quickly pointed out the flaws in Watson and Crick's model. DNA's tendency to soak up water meant that the phosphates had to be on the outside. Furthermore, their arrangement of the bases on the outside was far too unstable. She did not try to hide her amusement at their inside-out model, but did explain her experimental work to them. Franklin's response humbled Watson and Crick, but did not discourage them. Crick later admitted that he had not "known enough chemistry" to do the model correctly. Watson had also misunderstood the information he had heard at Franklin's earlier seminar. He thought she spoke of a low water content. He would not make that mistake again.

Watson and Crick's inside-out model only reinforced Franklin's conviction that it was foolish to try to build a model prematurely, based on hypothesis and conjecture. Models were valuable only if they allowed a structure to emerge from hard facts and verifiable data.

Aside from embarrassing them, Watson and Crick's hasty foray into DNA also announced their intentions of entering the arena that had been given to King's. No one, with the exception of Watson and Crick, wanted a race between King's and the Cavendish lab, and Wilkins wrote to Crick gently urging him to back off DNA research. The MRC, unwilling to fund the same project twice, also got involved. Randall contacted Sir Lawrence Bragg, the head of the Cavendish lab, who told Watson and Crick in no uncertain terms that they were to leave DNA research to King's.

Unfortunately, King's was making relatively little progress. Although a new camera for Wilkins was finally ready, he still could not get the Chargaff DNA to crystallize. Franklin, in the meantime, was looking for another job. Though she had by this time moved out of her parent's place, she had been unhappy during her time at King's and was ready for a change. On one occasion, Franklin arrived at her brother Colin's home for dinner, sobbing inconsolably. As he did not want to pry, he pretended not to notice.

Franklin traveled to Paris at the end of 1951 in the hopes of getting her old job back, but she changed her mind when she considered her career prospects there. She visited Vittorio Luzzati, her old friend and colleague from her Paris days, and showed him her diffraction photographs. Vittorio advised her to use Patterson function analysis to interpret them. This method uses information about the intensities of diffracted X-ray beams to produce a vector map of the structure. Such deductive work required intense mathematical calculations in order to produce a contoured maplike glimpse of the internal structure of the molecule. Franklin decided to return to King's and give the method a try. It suited her meticulous nature and mathematical skills.

By early 1952 Franklin was back in London. She gave her future some more thought and went to see J. D. Bernal, a pioneer of X-ray crystallography and the head of Birkbeck College's physics department. Franklin had applied to Birkbeck before but had been denied. Bernal now tentatively offered her a position at his lab in London. Franklin accepted, but agreed to stay at King's for the time being.

Wilkins, in the meantime, was still trying to hunt down adequate DNA samples. He contacted Professor Signer in Switzerland, who had first given him the samples at the conference in Berne. Signer invited Wilkins to his lab but misunderstood his reason for coming. He had no more DNA—he had given it all away at the conference and had no immediate plans to make more. Wilkins then went to the Stazione in Naples to get some more sepia sperm, which had given him some good DNA samples to work with in the past. There, he finally obtained some worthy samples, which, in turn, yielded clear photographs. Wilkins's diffraction images had patterns that strongly suggested a helical structure for DNA.

Unable to contain his enthusiasm, Wilkins wrote to Francis Crick to tell him of his new findings and to invite him to lunch to discuss it further. Wilkins did not honor the restrictions imposed on DNA research at the Cavendish lab. He may have felt he was merely sharing news that would be of interest to an old friend, the rare person who could appreciate the nature of his work.

Meanwhile, Franklin and Gosling continued photographing single DNA fibers from different angles at very close range, as close as 15 millimeters. A single exposure could last one hundred hours. Sometimes, the DNA fiber would transform from the A to the B form during its long hours of X-ray exposure, literally jumping out of the camera's focus as it changed shape.

Franklin finally began to settle into her life in London. She adored her new apartment, and frequently invited relatives, friends, and even some of her colleagues from the lab to dinner. She grew especially close to Gosling and his wife. At home, in her own element, Franklin was warm, thoughtful, and witty, almost the opposite of the somber, withdrawn scientist she was at work.

At the lab, Franklin and Gosling began to apply the Patterson functions to the photographs of the A form they were concentrating on, as per Franklin's agreement with Randall and Wilkins. Franklin was pretty sure

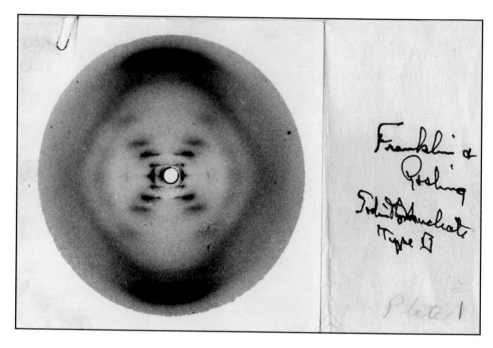

Franklin and Gosling's Photo 51. In accounts of the race to discover DNA's structure, Franklin's contribution is often restricted to providing this photo. (King's College, London)

that the B form was a helix shape, but she had strong doubts about the dry, crystalline A form. The photos she took of the A were sharper than those of the B, but also more confusing. When she applied the Patterson function analysis to the photos, the results were confusing and inconclusive. She had better samples and a better camera, but she was assigned the more difficult form of DNA to study.

In May of 1952, Franklin's camera captured the sharpest, clearest photo of the B form ever taken. The image showed a dominant black cross, an X standing alone, free of any other patterns, that was clearly the shape of a helix. With some basic mathematical calculations, the vital parameters of its structure could be determined. Franklin named their latest breakthrough "Photo 51." She and Gosling put it aside for the present, though, and redoubled their efforts at exploring the A form, as her agreement with Randall and Wilkins dictated.

After a trip to Yugoslavia in May to lecture and visit coal research facilities, Franklin told Randall of her plan to transfer to the crystallographic laboratory at Birkbeck. Randall approved the transfer but gave Franklin six more months to wrap up her research at King's.

Franklin and Gosling used this time to continue working with Patterson function analysis techniques. "We spent *ages*," Gosling recalled. We had to think in three dimensions." Franklin became convinced that A-form DNA was not a helix. She even wrote Wilkins and Stokes a witty mock invitation to a "memorial service" for the helix in A-form DNA:

> It is with great regret that we have to announce the death, on Friday 18th July, 1952, of D.N.A. Helix (crystalline).
>
> Death followed a protracted illness which an intensive course of Bessel injections had failed to relieve.
>
> A memorial service will be held next Monday or Tuesday. It is hoped that Dr. H.H.F. Wilkins will speak in memory of the late Helix.

But Franklin was wrong. The A-form diffraction photos, which were almost indecipherable, had mislead her. Franklin and Gosling's hours of long, painstaking calculations ultimately led them down a dead end.

six

THE DOUBLE HELIX

Late in 1952, Franklin was preparing to leave King's to take up her new position at the Birkbeck College laboratory in London. She was due to begin her new job in mid-March of 1953 and busily tried to finish up as much work as she could before leaving. She worked on three research papers with Gosling to be given to Randall before she left. Randall had decreed that she was to leave behind not only her DNA research, but all of her thoughts and ideas about DNA as well.

Wilkins was counting the days until she left. He planned to duplicate Franklin's data and launch "a general offensive on Nature's secret strongholds on all fronts: models, theoretical chemistry and interpretation of data crystalline and comparative," he wrote to Watson and Crick at the Cavendish lab.

Watson and Crick had become somewhat sidetracked, though. Peter Pauling, the great Linus Pauling's son, had come to the Cavendish lab to work on protein structure. The three young men soon became friends. Peter told Crick that his father had, for some time, been researching the supercoiling of alpha helices in protein molecules. Crick had been privately working on the same subject for the past year, and he scrambled to put together his findings and publish before Pauling did. Watson, meanwhile, had decided to build on research conducted by Joshua Lederberg on the genetics of bacteria.

Watson and Crick did not abandon all thoughts of DNA, however. They kept returning to discussion of biochemist and DNA pioneer Erwin Chargaff's discoveries about the nitrogen bases in DNA samples. Adenine and thymine quantities were always the same, as were guanine and cytosine quantities. No one had managed to explain Chargaff's findings, but they were clearly important to understanding the nature of DNA.

Another question connected to the structure of DNA was how DNA replicates itself when a cell splits. Though his thinking was not fully developed, Crick thought that the nitrogen bases in the DNA molecule (adenine, thymine, guanine and cytosine) could form complementary pairs and that the DNA molecule would effectively "unzip" when the cell divided. One base would pair up with its counterpart, forming a template, like a negative mold, from which to reconstruct an exact replica of the original DNA molecule. Crick also realized that the base pair

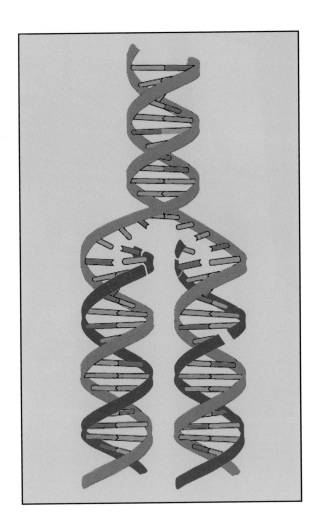

A strand of DNA replicating. The helix separates at the juncture of the base pairs, and two new helices are formed.

arrangement might explain how genes themselves were encoded. Different arrangements of the base pairs on the DNA molecule would translate into various traits—the arrangements constituted the "code of life." Others thought the bases repeated themselves and that the molecule copied itself directly, one nitrogen base into another of the same kind. Crick asked the theoretical chemist John Griffith to work out how the bases would pair up chemically. Griffith tentatively proposed that adenine and thymine chemically paired, as did guanine and cytosine.

James Watson, an American from Illinois, came to the Cavandish Laboratory to work on some postdoctoral research. (Courtesy of Getty Images.)

Around the time Franklin was arranging her departure from King's, Watson and Crick heard that Chargaff would be visiting Cambridge. They were part of a small group that joined him for drinks. Chargaff, however, immediately disliked the enthusiastic duo. It was not uncommon for Watson's gawky, unkempt persona to estrange him from colleagues. The garrulous Crick—"an incessant falsetto with occasional nuggets glittering in the turbid streams of prattle," as Chargaff described him—unwittingly revealed in the course of their conversation that he did not even know the chemical composition of the four bases in DNA. Chargaff quickly dismissed them as a pair of charlatans. Watson and Crick never collaborated with Chargaff, though his findings would help to confirm their final discovery.

Crick wanted to attempt another model, but Watson felt that without any new information it would be a waste of time and energy. The Chargaff discovery was promising, but they could not put together all of the pieces. They were at an impasse and would make no further progress until the beginning of February.

In December of 1952, Peter Pauling came to Watson with exciting news. His father had written him a letter from Cal Tech announcing that he and his collaborator, Robert Corey, had found the structure of DNA. Watson and Crick, dumbfounded, passed the letter back and forth, reading and rereading its contents. The letter did not specify what the structure was or how Pauling had found it. Crick suggested that they would still be entitled to equal credit if they found the structure before Pauling published his findings, but the news was a devastating blow. They clung to the slim possibility that Pauling had made a mistake.

Pauling sent a copy of the paper announcing his findings to Sir Lawrence Bragg, his old rival and the head of the Cavendish Laboratory, and another to his son Peter. When Peter brought the manuscript to the Cavendish Laboratory, Watson could hardly contain himself. He tore it from Peter's pocket and read. What he read astonished and delighted him.

Pauling had suggested a three-stranded helix with the phosphates on the inside—the same mistake Watson and Crick had made over a year ago. Additionally, to Watson's amazement, Pauling's proposed composition of the nucleic acid was not even chemically an acid. He had made a chemical error so basic that a college chemistry student could have caught it. Apparently the rush to be the first had resulted in some sloppy work. Watson speculated that no one at Cal Tech, where "Linus was like the Pope," had the courage to question his chemistry. According to his son, Pauling later said he had just "temporarily lost his marbles."

Pauling's faulty findings were soon to be published in a scientific journal. Crick and Watson knew this meant Pauling would be informed of his error immediately, almost certainly causing him to redouble his efforts for success. They knew he was quite capable of it. Crick and Watson estimated that they had roughly six weeks to crack the genetic code before Pauling did. They sped to the Eagle, their favorite pub, to "drink a toast to the Pauling failure," Watson said. "Though the odds still appeared against us, Linus had not yet won his Nobel." Ironically, Pauling never realized his error until after he saw Watson and Crick's final model.

Still at an impasse with their model building, Crick and Watson were in need of new data—anything to put them on a different track. Watson began loitering around King's in the hopes of running into Wilkins, much to the chagrin of several researchers there, including Franklin.

Once, when Franklin was at work in her room, the door swung open. Lurking in the doorway was Watson, who quickly engaged her in a conversation about Pauling's paper and the structure of DNA. They began to argue, and he implied that she was incompetent in interpreting X-ray photographs and needed to learn some theory. He described her reaction in *The Double Helix:*

> Suddenly Rosy came from behind the lab bench that separated us and began moving toward me. Fearing that in her hot anger she might strike me, I grabbed up the Pauling manuscript and hastily retreated to the open door. My escape was blocked by Wilkins, who, searching for me, had just then stuck his head through.

When Franklin left King's, Gosling was supposed to revert to Wilkins as his thesis supervisor. As part of this changeover, Gosling brought Wilkins all the research he had been involved in with Franklin, including Photo 51. This was the first time Wilkins had seen the photo, taken some eight months earlier, which showed an indisputable helical structure for the B form of DNA.

After Watson's run-in with Franklin at the King's lab, he and Wilkins grew closer. Watson had naturally heard about how Franklin had commandeered Wilkins's best camera and samples; now he had his own "Rosy" story to tell. As they commiserated about her one day, the unsuspecting Wilkins showed Photo 51 to Watson as an example of the superior images Franklin had been able to get with her camera. Watson's jaw dropped. The clarity of the image was truly unprecedented. With only a few calculations, anyone trained in crystallography could calculate the defining characteristics of the helix.

Unaware that Watson and Crick were poised for another model-building effort, Wilkins freely discussed King's other findings. The two went out for dinner together, and Watson pumped Wilkins for data to explain the photo he had just seen. Wilkins told him that the length of one turn of the helix was 34.4 angstroms (one angstrom equals one ten-billionth of a meter), and that this was ten times the spacing between the bases, stacked 3.4 angstroms apart. Wilkins had long been confident that DNA was helical but had been unable to figure out how the bases were packed inside the helix.

Armed with this new information, Watson rushed to ask Sir Lawrence Bragg about lifting the DNA moratorium at the Cavendish lab. He told Bragg that Pauling, who had already bested the Cavendish lab in discovering the structure of the alpha helix, would surely throw himself at DNA as soon as he realized his mistake. Bragg cringed at the thought of another Pauling victory over British laboratories, simply because of some interpersonal nonsense at King's. The moratorium on DNA research at the Cavendish Laboratory had been in place for more than a year and it seemed that there was little progress. It was time to end it. Bragg authorized the building of another model and put the entire resources of the Cavendish Laboratory at Watson and Crick's disposal.

It took three days for the machine shop to construct the model of the phosphorus and base molecules to their specifications, but once some of the pieces were ready, Watson began to string together sections for a phosphate-sugar backbone in the center. He resisted moving the bases to the inside because it would present the problem of how to pack irregular sequences of bases into either two or three chains.

Crick still believed there should be three chains, but Watson argued for two, with the chains of phosphates at the core. After days of attempting to arrange the model that way, an internal backbone did not seem to be working out. Watson decided to begin a model with the chains on the outside, as Franklin had suggested in 1951. The machine shop had not yet finished the flat plates cut in the base shapes, so he had the luxury of not having to deal with them for a short period.

Eager for any new information, Watson and Crick asked Max Perutz for a copy of the minutes of the December 1952 MRC meeting, which included an update of Franklin's research findings. The report was not confidential, so Perutz handed it over. In Franklin's summary, she noted that the A-form DNA was in the space group "monolithic C2." Crystals are classified into 230 space groups, depending on the shape of their unit cell. Franklin had overlooked this discovery at the time, but its significance did not escape Crick. He immediately realized that if the DNA crystal belonged to that particular space group, it was symmetrical and would look the same turned upside down. One chain of the helix must run up, while the other ran down. They would run antiparallel.

While Crick and Watson continued to work on their model, Franklin contemplated one of her own. She was still bogged down in the complicated A form and convinced that it was not a helix. She considered a figure eight with one chain crossing over on itself in repeating eights, and a paired-rod structure, eventually ruling both out. Out of time at King's, she dropped the work and returned to preparing her papers for publication.

Meanwhile, Crick and Watson still faced a number of problems. If the phosphate chains were on the outside, what would hold them together? And how would the bases, each with a different shape and size, fit between the chains? The bigger bases would overlap, while the smaller bases opposite each other would leave gaps, causing the chains to cave in. Impatient for the Cavendish lab machine shop to finish up the model bases, Watson made some of his own out of cardboard. He began moving them about, looking for an arrangement that would square with Franklin's measurements from her MRC summary report.

Watson began to propose a two-chained model with identical bases held together on the inside by hydrogen bonds. This arrangement would slightly warp the chains, since the bases would not be the same size from pair to pair on the rungs, but it seemed to fit. Watson explained his theory to the American crystallographer Jerry Donohue, who had been sharing Watson and Crick's office for the past half year. Donohue was a graduate student of Pauling's and an expert in hydrogen bonds. He informed Watson that he was using the incorrect form of the bases. The widely accepted "enol" form taught in many organic chemistry textbooks was, in fact, unlikely in this case. The bases would probably be in the recently discovered "keto" form, which had different bonding sites for hydrogen atoms.

Watson soon scrapped the like-with-like base pairing arrangement, especially after Crick pointed out that it did not conform to Chargaff's rules of adenine equaling thymine, and guanine equaling cytosine. Watson had been hesitant to use Chargaff's data, for an admittedly foolish reason: "I didn't like Chargaff, ever since I had met him a year before, I thought I don't want to use his data in finding the structure . . . boy, it was really stupid."

By the third week in February 1953, Franklin had concluded that the A and B forms were both helices, each composed of two chains. She had no problem accepting the work of Chargaff, as well as the idea of complementary base pairs. Later analysis of her notebooks and data would suggest that she was close to the final answer, but her career plans intervened. Her work at King's was done, and she left behind all thoughts of DNA to work for J. D. Bernal at Birkbeck Laboratory.

Meanwhile, Watson and Crick forged ahead. They knew the "pitch" of the helix from what Wilkins had showed and told them of Photo 51, and they had deduced the double, antiparallel chains from Franklin's report to the MRC. They now began switching the bases around on the inside of the helix. In the course of trial and error, they soon

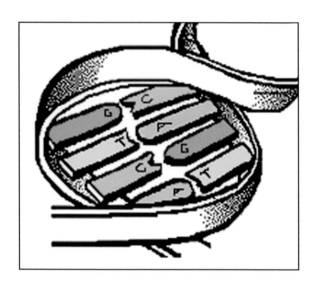

The base pairs of DNA follow a set pattern. Guanine and cytosine always pair together, as do adenine and thymine.

realized what Griffith had suggested the previous year and what Chargaff's discovery confirmed: adenine and thymine paired on the inside of the helix, as did guanine and cytosine. The arrangement seemed to fit. "All the hydrogen bonds seemed to form naturally, no fudging was required to make the two types of base pairs identical in shape," Watson said. The geometry of each of the pairs was almost identical. Furthermore, both base pairs could fit either way between the chains.

Suddenly, the model was complete. Watson and Crick had revealed the structure of DNA and had also inferred a great deal about how DNA replicates itself.

DNA is a double helix, like a twisted ladder with the phosphates and sugar molecules (the legs of the ladder) on the outside and the bases on the inside (the rungs). Each chain of the helix is an upside-down negative of the other. The base pairs carry the chemical instructions, and the order of the base pairs spells out the code, which in turn gives the genetic information for protein synthesis. Whenever one of the bases appears on the chain, its complement always faces it along the opposite strand. When the chains separate during replication, each single chain takes one

James Watson (sitting) and Francis Crick (gesturing with the pointer) show off their DNA model. (Courtesy of A. Barrington Brown / Photo Researchers, Inc.)

row of bases with it and forms a template from which to create another complementary chain of sugar-phosphate nucleotides and bases.

The code had been cracked by two scientists who had never conducted a single experiment, taken one X-ray photo, or looked at a single DNA fiber through a microscope. They had gathered the collective knowledge of a number of scientists and made a remarkable imaginative leap.

Watson and Crick kept their discovery quiet until a three-dimensional model of the molecule could be built, checked, measured, and firmly established. But once they made the anouncement, the news spread quickly within scientific circles. Using Franklin's data, they knew what the helix's measurements were, enabling them to build their model with the correct helical pitch (34A) and with the bases spaced at 3.4A. Her data also gave them the slope of the helix at 40 degrees and the diameter of the molecule at 20A. They made sure their model reflected these calculations.

Both Watson and Crick were embarrassed to tell Wilkins. As they stood admiring their model, they received an excited letter from him anticipating Franklin's departure and gearing up for a joint collaboration on DNA. "I think you will be interested to know that our dark lady leaves us next week. . . . At last the decks are clear and we can put all hands to the pumps!" he wrote. When he saw the model, Wilkins seemed genuinely excited that they had made such a significant breakthrough, but he was clearly disappointed that he had been left out. They offered him coauthorship of the paper they were about to publish describing the model, but he refused.

Actual experimental X-ray data from King's soon confirmed the likely validity of Crick and Watson's double helix model. Franklin herself immediately recognized that they had gotten it right. All who saw the model noted the beauty and simplicity of its logic. Raymond Gosling said:

> When you looked at this thing it was its elegant simplicity that hit you, this specific pairing, these steps across, a sort of lighthouse staircase of the model, you just felt that the ancient Greeks were absolutely right where if you wanted to say which was the better theorem you chose the most elegant one.

Watson and Crick rushed to write up a short paper and publish their results in order to claim precedence. The scientific journal *Nature* was the obvious choice for the speed with which it accepted and published manuscripts. The article was so hastily written that Crick later admitted, "The structure is produced like a rabbit out of a hat, with no indication as to how we arrived at it."

Randall was outraged by Watson and Crick's discovery. The Cavendish lab had scooped King's—the largest biophysics lab in Britain—in an area that was supposed to be exclusively theirs. He wanted to make sure that his lab at least got credit for the DNA work it had done. He convinced the editors of *Nature* to postpone the publication of Watson and Crick's article for a few weeks to give King's an opportunity to submit its own article about

We wish to thank Prof. J. T. Randall for encouragement ; Profs. E. Chargaff, R. Signer, J. A. V. Butler and Drs. J. D. Watson, J. D. Smith, L. Hamilton, J. C. White and G. R. Wyatt for supplying material without which this work would have been impossible ; also Drs. J. D. Watson and Mr. F. H. C. Crick for stimulation, and our colleagues R. E. Franklin, R. G. Gosling, G. L. Brown and W. E. Seeds for discussion. One of us (H. R. W.) wishes to acknowledge the award of a University of Wales Fellowship.

M. H. F. WILKINS
Medical Research Council Biophysics
Research Unit,

A. R. STOKES
H. R. WILSON
Wheatstone Physics Laboratory,
King's College, London.
April 2.

[1] Astbury, W. T., Symp. Soc. Exp. Biol., 1, Nucleic Acid (Cambridge Univ. Press, 1947).
[2] Riley, D. P., and Oster, G., Biochim. et Biophys. Acta, 7, 526 (1951).
[3] Wilkins, M. H. F., Gosling, R. G., and Seeds, W. E., Nature, 167, 759 (1951).
[4] Astbury, W. T., and Bell, F. O., Cold Spring Harb. Symp. Quant. Biol., 6, 109 (1938).
[5] Cochran, W., Crick, F. H. C., and Vand, V., Acta Cryst., 5, 581 (1952).
[6] Wilkins, M. H. F., and Randall, J. T., Biochim. et Biophys. Acta, 10, 192 (1953).

Molecular Configuration in Sodium Thymonucleate

SODIUM thymonucleate fibres give two distinct types of X-ray diagram. The first corresponds to a crystalline form, structure A, obtained at about 75 per cent relative humidity ; a study of this is described in detail elsewhere[1]. At higher humidities a different structure, structure B, showing a lower degree of order, appears and persists over a wide range of ambient humidity. The change from A to B is reversible. The water content of structure B fibres which undergo this reversible change may vary from 40–50 per cent to several hundred per cent of the dry weight. Moreover, some fibres never show structure A, and in these structure B can be obtained with an even lower water content.

The X-ray diagram of structure B (see photograph) shows in striking manner the features characteristic of helical structures, first worked out in this laboratory by Stokes (unpublished) and by Crick, Cochran and Vand[5]. Stokes and Wilkins were the first to propose such structures for nucleic acid as a result of direct studies of nucleic acid fibres, although a helical structure had been previously suggested by Furberg (thesis, London, 1949) on the basis of X-ray studies of nucleosides and nucleotides.

While the X-ray evidence cannot, at present, be taken as direct proof that the structure is helical, other considerations discussed below make the existence of a helical structure highly probable.

Structure B is derived from the crystalline structure A when the sodium thymonucleate fibres take up quantities of water in excess of about 40 per cent of their weight. The change is accompanied by an increase of about 30 per cent in the length of the fibre, and by a substantial re-arrangement of the molecule. It therefore seems reasonable to suppose that in structure B the structural units of sodium thymonucleate (molecules on groups of molecules) are relatively free from the influence of neighbouring

Sodium deoxyribose nucleate from calf thymus. Structure B

molecules, each unit being shielded by a sheath of water. Each unit is then free to take up its least-energy configuration independently of its neighbours and, in view of the nature of the long-chain molecules involved, it is highly likely that the general form will be helical[2]. If we adopt the hypothesis of a helical structure, it is immediately possible, from the X-ray diagram of structure B, to make certain deductions as to the nature and dimensions of the helix.

The innermost maxima on the first, second, third and fifth layer lines lie approximately on straight lines radiating from the origin. For a smooth single-strand helix the structure factor on the nth layer line is given by :

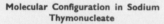

$$F_n = J_n(2\pi rR) \exp i\, n(\psi + \tfrac{1}{2}\pi),$$

where $J_n(u)$ is the nth-order Bessel function of u, r is the radius of the helix, and R and ψ are the radial and azimuthal co-ordinates in reciprocal space[2]; this expression leads to an approximately linear array of intensity maxima of the type observed, corresponding to the first maxima in the functions J_1, J_2, J_3, etc.

If, instead of a smooth helix, we consider a series of residues equally spaced along the helix, the transform in the general case treated by Crick, Cochran and Vand is more complicated. But if there is a whole number, m, of residues per turn, the form of the transform is as for a smooth helix with the addition, only, of the same pattern repeated with its origin at heights mc^*, $2mc^*$ . . . etc. (c is the fibre-axis period).

In the present case the fibre-axis period is 34 A. and the very strong reflexion at 3·4 A. lies on the tenth layer line. Moreover, lines of maxima radiating from the 3·4-A. reflexion as from the origin are visible on the fifth and lower layer lines, having a J_5 maximum coincident with that of the origin series on the fifth layer line. (The strong outer streaks which apparently radiate from the 3·4-A. maximum are not, however, so easily explained.) This suggests strongly that there are exactly 10 residues per turn of the helix. If this is so, then from a measurement of R_n the position of the first maximum on the nth layer line (for $n < 5$), the radius of the helix, can be obtained. In the present instance, measurements of R_1, R_2, R_3 and R_5 all lead to values of r of about 10 A.

Photo 51 (seen in the top right corner) debuted in the April 1953 issue of Nature. Up to this point, no one outside of King's should have seen it. (Ebsco) the DNA X-ray work. The editors decided to publish the Cavendish lab and King's articles side by side in the April 25, 1953, issue.

Watson and Crick's short article titled "A Structure for Deoxyribose Nucleic Acid" appeared first, describing their proposed structure. They ended the article with a famous understatement: "It has not escaped our notice that the specific pairing we have postulated immediately suggests a possible copying mechanism for the genetic material." Next came Wilkins's article, which lent experimental support to Watson and Crick's theory of a double-helix structure. Lastly, Franklin and Gosling's article, written before Watson and Crick announced their discovery, described many of the helical parameters that had in fact been so central for Watson and Crick. Franklin's article was presented as mere background support for the groundbreaking findings of Watson and Crick, rather than the foundation and spring-board for their discovery. She had no idea that Watson and Crick had seen her data, particularly Photo 51.

Watson and Crick were in the unenviable position of hav-ing the solution to one of the most perplexing questions in science, but without any experimental work to illustrate how they had figured it out. Their model was not fully validated until almost twenty years later. They had pulled together pieces of the puzzle from others' work and made brilliant, insightful connections to find the answer. Their influences were so wide and deep it presented a real problem: even if they wanted to credit the sources of all of their data, how could they? They could not mention Franklin's Photo 51, nor her MRC report. Both were unpublished and seen by them surreptitiously.

They dealt with the problem carefully in their paper. "The previously published X-ray data on deoxyribose nucleic acid are insufficient for a rigorous test of our structure," they wrote. "We were not aware of the details of the results presented there when we devised our structure, which rests mainly though not entirely on published experimental data and stereochemical arguments." Their statement was borderline dishonest. They had not seen the drafts of the articles that would appear in *Nature* alongside theirs, but they had come to know enough of the King's data and details to base their work on it.

"We are much indebted to Dr. Jerry Donohue for constant advice and criticism, especially on inter-atomic distances," the pair wrote at the end of their historic paper. "We have also been stimulated by a knowledge of the general nature of the unpublished experimental results and ideas of Dr. M. H. F. Wilkins, Dr. R. E. Franklin and their co-workers at King's College, London."

Even with the acknowledgement given him in their paper, Jerry Donohue considered his part in the discovery to be largely unrecognized. "Let's face it," he said. "If the fates hadn't ordained that I share an office with Watson and Crick in the Cavendish . . . they'd still be puttering around trying to pair 'like with like' enol forms of the bases."

Though she never found out that Watson and Crick had used her data, Franklin never showed signs of bitterness that her hard-earned experimental work was lost amid the chorus of cheers that heralded Watson and Crick's discovery. Her sister, Jenifer, even said, "I do not remember her feeling that she had lost a competition, only that something exciting had been discovered, and that she longed now to work somewhere more congenial."

Franklin saw Crick and Watson's model as a confirmation of her work, which she realized validated their model. She likely never suspected that their model was built significantly on her work.

When Franklin left King's she did not look back. She had yet to do the finest scientific work of her life.

seven

A LIFE CUT SHORT

After vacationing in the newly founded Jewish State of Israel, Franklin began her new job. The equipment and facilities at Birkbeck College were far inferior to what she had worked with at King's. Franklin described the move as going from "a palace to a slum." The college's brick buildings had barely survived the bombings of the war; many were still damaged or had been hastily repaired. Franklin's little office was on the fifth floor, in what was formerly a maid's room, and the X-ray equipment was located in the basement. A narrow, twisted staircase led to the floors below. The roof leaked in the lab, an old converted kitchen. Franklin put out beakers to catch the drips and unfurled an umbrella while setting up her equipment.

The scientists who occupied the lab were much more impressive than where they worked. The head of the physics

department at Birkbeck was the Irish-born crystallographer
J. D. Bernal. Nicknamed "Sage" as a college undergraduate, Bernal was not only a brilliant scientist but also an
intellectual, renowned for his near-omniscience in almost
every subject. A biographer once asked Bernal to think of
a subject unfamiliar to him. He replied "eighth-century
Romanian churches," but called back several days later to
change his answer to "sixth-century Romanian churches."
During the war, he had helped plan the Allied invasion of
France. He was an outspoken political leftist. His political
beliefs, though slightly annoying to the more moderate
Franklin, led him to cultivate an egalitarian atmosphere
in his lab that was much to her liking. Like John Randall
at King's, Bernal had a knack for surrounding himself
with scientific talent and ample research money. Franklin
considered him a good boss.

In 1948, Bernal had set up the Biomolecular Research
Laboratory at Birkbeck to resume research he had started
before the war on plant viruses and large molecules. He
tried to set up a separate crystallography department but
was rebuffed by the Master of Birkbeck, who decided the
physics department already enjoyed an unfair share of the
school's resources.

At Birkbeck Franklin researched the tobacco mosaic
virus (TMV), which was responsible for the destruction
of hundreds of types of plant crops worldwide. The virus
got its name from the mottled, or mosaic, patches of green,
yellow, and white it causes on the leaves of infected plants.
It rarely kills the plant, but stunts its growth. Scientists

The tobacco mosaic virus, one of the most common and virulent of all plant diseases, can live for fifty years on dead plant material. Even dipping contaminated gardening tools in bleach will not prevent its spread. (Clemson University - USDA Cooperative Extension Slide Series)

knew that the virus contains proteins and the nucleic acid RNA. RNA was closely related to DNA, but less was known about it. Franklin's team hoped finding the structure of the TMV virus would reveal important information about the function and behavior of it and other viruses.

It was already understood that when the virus enters a host cell, it takes over the metabolic processes rather than killing it. The virus has no cell of its own. It is simply genetic material, somewhere between living and dead matter, without any chemical or physiological properties.

Once it takes over a cell, the virus multiplies and spreads to other cells, both within the same plants and to different plants. It invades other plants through small scratches in the surface, often made by chewing insects.

In 1936, Norman Pirie and Frederick Bawden had discovered that TMV was rod-shaped (viruses are either rod-shaped or spherical). TMV was a good model for studying other viruses because it was relatively stable and easy to culture in a lab. Studies by Bernal and others had later shown that it was made up of identical protein subunits and RNA, but no one knew how they were arranged.

James Watson had also studied TMV at the Cavendish lab when he and Crick were prohibited from DNA work. He had determined that these subunits were helical, but had abandoned TMV research when he realized it would require intensive, in-depth experimentation and would not likely yield quick or easy dividends. Franklin, undeterred by slow, painstaking, experimental science, stepped up to the challenge. She went to work taking X-ray diffraction photographs of the virus in its crystalline form. Almost immediately, Franklin realized that TMV's secrets would be more elusive than those of DNA, because the X-ray patterns were very difficult to analyze.

In early 1954, only a few months after Franklin had begun her research at Birkbeck, she was invited to participate in a summer coal research conference to be held in New Hampshire. She had never been to the United States. She planned a two-month trip to visit several industrial and biological labs, from the Massachusetts Institute of

Technology (MIT) in Boston to the Virus Laboratory at the University of California at Berkeley.

Franklin was leery of the United States. She distrusted what she saw as the materialism and arrogance in American life. After the New Hampshire coal conference, she began her tours of laboratories. At MIT, a nucleic acids specialist offered to drive her to the Marine Biological Laboratory in Woods Hole on Cape Cod, where she witnessed a hurricane on her first day. There she ran into James Watson, who was also visiting Woods Hole and was now a Senior Research Fellow in Biology at Cal Tech. She and Watson got along better than they had in England and had some fruitful conversations about TMV. He even offered her a ride across the country to California, but she declined. She had a full agenda ahead of her.

After briefly visiting New York and Philadelphia, Franklin headed west to give lectures on her coal research and to continue touring the biological labs. She wrote home:

> My lab visits were in two curiously interesting groups. In the carbon world the work I did in Paris seems to form the background to a large part of the industrial research going on here, and I'm welcomed as an "authority" on the subject. . . . In the biological laboratories, on the other hand, I have much to learn and almost nothing to give, and it is a question of hunting out the people who enjoy wasting their time talking to me. The contrast between the two groups of people I meet is also very striking. The carbon crowd are entirely uninspired, but in the biological

laboratories there are an impressive number of really first-class people.

As she traveled west and stayed with various hosts, Franklin warmed up to everyday American people. Upon reaching the West Coast, she visited the University of California at Los Angeles (UCLA), Cal Tech, and Berkeley. She gave a talk on X-rays of TMV crystals and saw Linus Pauling, as well as Watson. Watson told her of the newest TMV research, conducted by a Yale scientist named Don Caspar, that seemed to suggest that the core of the virus was hollow, rather than filled with RNA.

During their free time, Watson and another Cal Tech scientist showed Franklin around some of the seedier sections of Hollywood and Los Angeles. She wrote home that "The centre of Hollywood is vulgar and characterless, and only a little less sordid than the centre of Los Angeles." Despite occasional flurries of disapproval, Franklin liked American people, especially the scientists she met at the universities. She found them competent, dedicated, and congenial.

When she returned to England, Franklin continued to form attachments to most of her new colleagues. It was a much different working environment that King's had been. She especially meshed with Aaron Klug, a Lithuanian-born physicist and chemist from South Africa. Largely a theoretician, he thought Franklin was a brilliant experimentalist. Their abilities complemented one another, and Franklin became close to Klug and his wife.

Aaron Klug, who went on to knighthood and to win a Nobel Prize in Chemistry, became Franklin's good friend and fellow virus enthusiast. Klug has remained one of Franklin's staunchest professional admirers. (AP Photo)

Franklin and Klug advertised for help in several scientific publications and eventually hired two doctoral students—John Finch, from King's, and Kenneth Holmes, from Cambridge. Franklin and Holmes worked on TMV and other rod-shaped viruses while Klug and Finch took on spherical viruses. Franklin led the research group, which was funded by the Agricultural Research Council (ARC), a government organization that played a critical role in the production of food through involvement in agribusiness and biotechnology. J. D. Bernal allowed Klug to work with Frankin's group, even though his funding was separate. They were a cohesive, productive unit.

Birkbeck proved to be a better situation than King's, but it was not a perfect fit for Franklin. She was still reserved and self-protective, awkward and shy in conversation. She could be forceful and demanding, and struck some of her colleagues the wrong way. Kenneth Holmes said that, "She was prickly and difficult, especially at first, unable to put people at their ease. There was a forcefulness about her manner . . . a barrier to be overcome if you wanted to get to know her." She was also a political moderate amid a sea of communists and left-wingers. Also, unlike almost everyone at Birkbeck, she came from a wealthy, upper-middle-class background.

Unlike her experience at King's, however, she was recognized as a distinguished scientist and admired by those who knew her well. "I would have gone through fire and water for her," said Holmes. Klug marveled at her experimental abilities. "She *noticed*," he later said. "She *noticed* everything. The fact that she produced the best specimens of TMV wasn't due to chance, or simple mechanical skills. It's an art, doing this, it's a matter of the pains she took, the way she nursed it, the keeping track of things, the *noticing*. That's how discoveries are made. And this was one of Rosalind's greatest gifts."

In late 1954, Franklin decided to compile her recent

data and photographs and publish a paper on her TMV research in *Nature.* She sent a copy of the article to British biochemist and prominent virologist Norman Pirie. Pirie had recently approved Franklin's grant from the ARC and provided her with several virus samples. He also had a reputation for being dismissive and rude to younger scientists. After reading Franklin's article he wrote a scathing letter blasting her claims that the TMV has a fixed, or uniform, length and that the subunits were all of the same type. He went so far as to imply she had done sloppy work.

Franklin wrote back and respectfully defended her research. She ended her letter with the hope that "you do not disapprove so strongly of what I have written that you will never again be willing to provide me with material to work on." She would have no such luck. Pirie was so offended that a young woman researcher had questioned him that he never sent her another virus specimen. Despite Pirie's temper tantrum, Franklin ultimately proved to be correct on both accounts.

In the summer of 1955 another important collaborator joined Franklin's group. Don Caspar, the American biophysicist who had discovered that TMV was hollow, wrote to Franklin to ask if he might work with her. She had no funding for him, but she told him he was welcome to come. He was twenty-seven years old, American, extremely bright, Jewish, and dedicated to TMV research. Franklin and Caspar instantly clicked.

Caspar suggested they use new techniques (called isomorphous replacement) created by Max Perutz, to give them

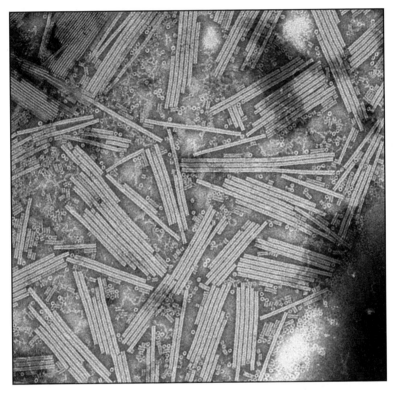

The hollow, tubular tobacco mosaic virus turned out to be just as Franklin conjectured. (T. Moravec)

clearer X-ray photos. With this technique they could see that the RNA in TMV was wrapped like a twisted string around the inner frame between the protein subunits. They were also able to determine the exact distance of the RNA from the center of the virus. To their delight, the structure of the virus revealed its behavior. The protein subunits protected the RNA strand by surrounding it. Once the virus got inside the host cell, the protein released the RNA, which then created a new virus. They had discovered how a viral infection occurred.

The next step was to build a three-dimensional model of TMV. They sent their technician to the local five-and-dime to see if he could find something that looked like protein subunits. He returned with almost 300 rubber handlebar grips and a funny story of the looks he got from the store employee who waited on him.

Over the next year, Franklin's team expanded its research to include many other plant viruses, and turned out numerous papers. Franklin frequently consulted with Francis Crick, who was still at the Cavendish Laboratory, and grew very close to him and his wife, Odile. She obtained virus samples from contacts she had made in the United States and elsewhere. Sometimes samples came from unexpected places. Once, Aaron Klug and Don Caspar used leftover crystals they found in the laboratory refrigerator from experiments Bernal had conducted before the war.

In spite of her group's success, Franklin was perpetually struggling with her funding agency, the ARC. She had a disastrous meeting with Sir William Slater, the secretary of the ARC and a close friend of Norman Pirie. Franklin asked for a promotion, a raise, and funding for Klug when his grant ran out. Slater treated her coldly and patronizingly, denying her every request. She left the meeting in tears.

Her funding woes notwithstanding, Franklin became more and more respected within her field. She received numerous invitations to scientific conferences throughout Europe and expanded her already large circle of professional contacts. In May of 1956, she traveled to the United States again for another two-month visit and symposium tour, to be paid for by the Rockefeller Foundation. She also went to seek out funding for her group, possibly from the U.S. National Institutes of Health. Don Caspar would be going too. He had been continuing his virus research at Yale University in Connecticut, and would attend many of the same conferences as Franklin.

As she traveled along her conference circuit, Franklin seemed to enjoy America even more this time around. She marveled at the high standard of living and the variety of food. At a conference in New Hampshire, she met a number of familiar faces, including Don Caspar and Sir Lawrence Bragg, who was now a resident professor at the Royal Institution. Bragg came with good news. The Royal Institution wanted Franklin to oversee the building of two large virus models representing her work at Birkbeck, which would be displayed at the upcoming Brussels World's Fair. The model would be housed in the International Science Hall Building for thousands of fairgoers to view.

Franklin started spending more time with Caspar. Caspar later said he had "more rapport with Rosalind than with most of the men I knew." They decided to meet up in Berkeley, and then again at his family's home in Colorado Springs.

Franklin's hosts on her second U.S. tour remembered a sweet, smiling, deeply humane woman. Those who had met her during her first trip who had found her to be a pushy, wound-up woman now saw her as good-humored, relaxed, and charming. After giving a seminar at Cal Tech, she went on a hiking trek up Mount Whitney. She and her

Franklin's striking TMV model must have attracted a great deal of attention at the Brussels World's Fair. The model can still be seen at the Laboratory of Molecular Biology at Cambridge. (Courtesy of MRC Laboratory of Molecular Biology, England.)

companions hiked all day and then camped under a rock ledge overnight. Watching the sun come up at dawn and play on the mountain summit, Franklin fell in love with southern California.

During her stay in California, Franklin felt sharp pains in her lower abdomen that continued over several days. She reluctantly visited a doctor, who gave her painkillers to alleviate the symptoms until she could see her regular doctor in London.

At Berkeley, Franklin received word from Don Caspar that his father had died and he would not be able to meet her. She was greatly disappointed and wrote her condolences to him, suggesting a possible meeting back east before she returned to London. A few days later, Caspar invited her to Colorado Springs again. She delayed her return by a week to visit him. Little is known of Franklin's relationship with Don, but several of Franklin's friends speculated that they were in love.

Back in New York, Franklin began to notice that her clothes no longer fit. Her stomach had a bulge. Nonetheless, she arrived in London on a Friday, as planned, and went straight to the lab to put in a full day's work. She promised herself to get medical attention within the next few days.

Franklin's doctor at first thought she was pregnant, and Franklin mused that she wished she were. A few days later, a surgeon at University College Hospital diagnosed Franklin's abdominal mass as ovarian cancer. She had two tumors, one on the right ovary "the size of a croquet ball" and another on the left, "tennis ball size."

Franklin's prognosis was not good. The cancer was already at a fairly advanced stage. Whether her work around X-ray radiation caused the cancer is unknown. Her family had a history of cancer, and many of her fellow male researchers did not contract the disease. But radiation exposure has been strongly linked to ovarian cancer.

Franklin underwent two surgeries within weeks, removing both of her ovaries and her uterus. At that point, the cancer seemed to be contained, and Franklin looked forward to regaining her strength and returning to the lab. She kept in touch with the lab from her parents' home and wrote up some of her notes while recuperating.

Most of Franklin's friends did not know the extent of her illness. At the lab, it was generally thought that she had a "female" problem. Franklin told several friends who used her apartment while she recuperated at her parents' house that she had just a minor operation and would be back to work shortly.

While Franklin's friend Anne Sayre was staying at her apartment, she answered the phone and heared Jacques Mering on the line. Jacques had not known of Franklin's second operation and became quite upset on hearing the news. When Franklin learned of his call, she, too, became very emotional, confessing that she had been in love with him.

Franklin did not like being an invalid at her parents' home. She had never developed an intimate relationship with her mother, whose anxiety over her illness now took the form of hand-wringing over her uneaten lunch or nagging her about getting more rest. Franklin became more withdrawn and noncommunicative. She eventually decided to leave her parents' care and arranged to stay with Francis and Odile Crick, who were always welcoming and did not intrude in her affairs.

In October of 1956, Franklin returned to Birkbeck. Feeling much better, she turned her attention to securing funding for her group. Distrustful of the ARC, she submitted a detailed application to the Public Health Service of the U.S. National Institutes of Health. In April of 1957, the ARC came through with a final year of financial support but stressed that it would not renew the grant next year. Franklin's group anxiously awaited word from the U.S.

Soon after, Franklin was rushed to the hospital with profuse bleeding. She stayed there for two days before being released, but was readmitted a few weeks later with intense abdominal pain. Examinations revealed that the cancer had returned. There was a new growth on the left side of her pelvis.

Franklin asked her surgeon for an honest appraisal of her condition. He told her she should prepare for death and seek the comforts of religion. Franklin was furious, primarily because she had so much work she wanted to complete. She planned to begin cobalt radiotherapy treatments, a new method that used ionizing radiation to kill cancer cells, but often without precision and in such a way that damaged the surrounding healthy tissue.

Returning to the lab, Franklin realized she needed to get going on the model building projects due in November for the Brussels World's Fair. A professor from the University of Chicago's microbiology unit was organizing the international science section of the Fair and told her to make their models as big as possible—at least five feet high—to wow the crowd. Her models were going to be the showpieces of the virus exhibit.

As she worked, Franklin hid her illness. Throughout her cobalt treatments in the summer of 1957, she was busily involved in several scientific exhibitions. At the Royal Society's *conversazione*, an annual natural history exhibition open to the public, Franklin stood presenting and explaining her work for hours at a time, masking any pain or fatigue. Her attending parents thought she looked happy and lovely.

In July she finally heard from the U.S. Public Health Service; they had approved her team's research grant. The grant would be for 10,000 pounds annually (around 28,000 American dollars) for each of three years. Some of her colleagues could have managed quite nicely on 10,000 pounds spread over the entire three years.

That summer, Don Caspar came to England with his mother. Franklin and Caspar renewed their friendship and later traveled to Switzerland for a vacation interspersed with scientific conferences. In Geneva they saw American doctor Jonas Salk speak on the polio vaccine, which he had invented four years earlier. Caspar's mother and a friend of his from Yale joined them for a weekend at the Alpine resort of Zermatt, at the foot of the majestic Matterhorn. Franklin did not mention her illness, but Don could not help but notice that she lacked the strength she had the previous summer.

She left them to attend a conference in Paris, and then

Franklin's friend from Paris, Vittorio Luzzati, took this picture of her looking out over Tuscany. (Supplied by Churchill Archives Centre, Cambridge, © Jenifer Glynn.)

met up with her sister Jenifer for a driving tour through northern Italy. She spent a day with the family of Vittorio Luzzati, an old friend from her Paris days. Franklin's easy-going manner and attractive appearance made a positive impression on Luzzati's mother, who expected a woman scientist to behave more like a staunch suffragette.

When she returned to Birkbeck, Franklin took up a new interest inspired by Jonas Salk: the polio virus. Two of her contacts from Berkeley offered to send her polio crystals. Unfortunately, some of the staff at Birkbeck felt uncomfortable having live polio virus around the lab. The old, dilapidated building was hardly set up to monitor and supervise infectious materials safely. The mere mention of the polio virus often elicited irrational responses among people during the 1950s. The disease had been dramatically curbed by Salk's vaccine, but memories lingered of the death and crippling that the disease had caused. A 1916 outbreak had left 6,000 dead and 27,000 paralyzed. Franklin knew it was dangerous, but they only risked exposure if a test tube broke. Undaunted, Franklin stored the live polio crystals for a time in a thermos flask in her parents' refrigerator. "You'll never guess what's in there," she said to her alarmed mother. "Live polio virus."

By mid-October, Bernal had found a home for the polio samples at the neighboring London School of Hygiene and Tropical Medicine. X-ray photographs of the crystals would be taken at the Royal Institution, not at Birkbeck, out of deference to the staff. Aaron Klug and John Finch, who would also be working with the polio virus, decided to get vaccinated as a precautionary measure. Franklin chose not to.

One month later Franklin was admitted to the Royal Marsden Hospital. The doctors drained her stomach of fluid and began her on a course of chemotherapy treatments. She liked the doctors at Royal Marsden. She was in and out of the hospital from November of 1957 to January of 1958. With the many friends and family who came to visit and stay by her bedside, she appeared cheerful, hopeful, and happy to chat. Ensconced in a single room at the end of the corridor, she continued her work from her bed, her papers and calculations spread all around her.

In January, she was whisked away from the hospital by her cousin Ursula for a day outing—a mission in search of good French food. Her spirits were so lifted by that day that Franklin decided to leave the hospital and continue treatments as an outpatient. By mid-January, she had signed a new three-year lease on her apartment and was showing up at the lab on a daily basis. She made bright fabric slipcovers for her apartment furniture, secured funds for her team to go to a conference in April, and began plans to take her summer holiday back in the United States.

In the back of Franklin's mind was the dull anxiety that the U.S. grant was a temporary stay of execution, that her group would simply disband after three years. She was therefore pleased when Max Perutz came to Birkbeck to offer Franklin's group a spot at a new laboratory dedicated for work in molecular biology opening at Cambridge. They were free to make the move as soon as their grant ran out. At last, the future of Franklin's group was secure.

Although weaker by the end of March, Franklin continued to frequent the lab. Often fatigued, she sometimes worked half-days. She would set things up, prepare her samples for X-ray photos, and calculate the data. She walked up and down five flights of stairs, without complaint, to get to her office and the lab. Even in Franklin's debilitated condition, her notebooks showed five pages of calculations for a single day.

On March 30, Franklin was readmitted to the hospital. The cancer had spread. Doctors tried a new chemotherapy treatment, but there was no improvement. She grew steadily weaker. Many friends and family members came to her bedside during her final two weeks, including Jacques Mering. He described Franklin as defiantly optimistic about her recovery, even as her body was almost skeletal. He confided his grief at her certain death, and remorse at his handling of her affections toward him.

On April 16th, 1958, newspapers carried stories of the Brussels World's Fair, with special mention for the scientific exhibits. Franklin's model detailing the molecular structure of a virus was prominently displayed, heralding a new era of scientific advances. Franklin died that same day. She was thirty-seven years old.

eight

THE LAST WORD

Franklin's short but distinguished career had a lasting effect on science. Her work on coal and viruses was significant, as well as her largely unsung contribution to the unlocking of the genetic code. Even within her lifetime, the reverberations of the DNA discovery began to be felt. The new fields of molecular genetics and molecular biology were born. Understanding of the inner-workings of the cell grew exponentially. In the years since her death, the advances have been even more dramatic. In 1961, Crick and Sydney Brenner discovered that the genetic code is actually written in triplets, with sets of three bases.

In 1986, the Human Genome Project was launched in an attempt to map all of the base pairs in the human genetic code. The project was concluded successfully in 2002. The practical applications of biogenetics have been manifold, from DNA forensics to genetically modified crops to "gene therapy" for curing genetic diseases. But the final implications of the "genetic revolution" are only beginning to be realized.

In 1962, Watson, Crick, and Wilkins were awarded the Nobel Prize in Physiology or Medicine for "discoveries concerning the molecular structure of nucleic acids and its significance for information transfer in living material." The Nobel Prize cannot be given posthumously, so Franklin was not eligible. No one can say whether she would have won if she had still been alive. History had largely passed over her role in DNA research as Watson and Crick took the lion's share of the credit.

But later in the decade, after the 1968 publication of Watson's *The Double Helix*, a movement began to see that Franklin received her due. Watson's book was an engaging, chatty narrative about the DNA discovery and quickly became a bestseller. His portrayal of Franklin as a frigid, aggressive shrew caused a backlash even before it was published. Watson's publisher, Harvard University Press, requested written consent from the book's principals before they agreed to print it. When Pauling, Perutz, Klug, Wilkins, and Crick (all of whom, incidentally, won Nobel Prizes) objected to Watson's portrayal of Franklin, Harvard University Press decided not to publish the book. Watson

Opposite: *A lineup of some of the Nobel Prize winners for 1962: (left to right) Professor Maurice Wilkins, Dr. Max Perutz, Dr. Francis Crick, John Steinbeck, Professor James Watson, and Dr. John C. Kendrew.* (Courtesy of Keystone / Getty Images.)

easily found another publisher, although he did add an epilogue qualifying some of the impressions of Franklin he made in the book. But the addendum did not erase the 223 pages that preceded it.

Several of the scientists who knew her spoke out in Franklin's defense after the book became famous, most notably Aaron Klug. But the runaway success of Watson's book seemed to ensure that she would be forever branded as the terrible "Rosy." Then, in 1971, Franklin's good friend Anne Sayre published a biography of Franklin in an attempt to set the record straight. With the women's movement gaining momentum in the 1970's, Sayre's account caught the attention of many feminists who seized on her story as an example of the type of condescension so many women faced in the workplace. Watson's blatantly chauvinist descriptions of Franklin only made their argument seem more plausible. She became, posthumously, something of a feminist icon.

Watson and Crick, who were both public figures, started facing increasingly pointed questions about Franklin and how they had obtained the data used in building the first DNA model. When it was revealed they had used some of Franklin's work without her consent or knowledge and had not credited her, they began to receive more criticism. Watson came under heavy fire for publicly maligning her character after she had died.

In 1982, Aaron Klug won the Nobel Prize in Chemistry for his development of crystallographic electron microscopy. In his Nobel lecture, he spoke admiringly of his former colleague. "It was Rosalind Franklin who set me the example of tackling large and difficult problems," he said. "Had her life not been cut tragically short, she might well have stood in this place on an earlier occasion."

In the years since publication of *The Double Helix*, biographies, television documentaries, and retrospective accounts by some of the key players in the DNA story have helped correct the record. Buildings at both Newnham College and King's have been named after Franklin. In a recent interview, Watson said that she should have been given the Nobel Prize for her experimental work on DNA.

Dr. Rosalind Franklin, pioneering DNA researcher and dedicated scientist. (Courtesy of Photo Researchers.)

No one can definitively say how close Franklin came to solving the DNA puzzle alone. She made important discoveries that were critical to Watson and Crick's model. However, it can not be denied that the final leaps the two men made were both brilliant and significant. Science sometimes progresses in great bounds, and Watson and Crick's decision to forge ahead with a model was one such step. They were brilliant scientists, and their accomplishment stands as a testament to the power of imaginative thinking.

But brilliance and imagination do not operate in a vacuum. Their breakthrough rested on a foundation of painstakingly harvested data and the experimentation of other scientists, Franklin chief among them. Experimentation was Franklin's great strength. Her friend Vittorio Luzzati later remarked on her "golden hands" that could design and execute elegant experiments. Scientists such as Watson and Crick are necessary to progress with their genius for cognitively piecing together evidence to form theories. But science also needs people like Franklin who do the work that informs, inspires and tests those theories. Theory alone is useless unless it can be tested and validated by hard, observable, repeatable experimentation and data. This was the power of Rosalind Franklin's talent and method. It is also the basis of modern science.

TIMELINE

1920	Born on July 25 in London.
1929	Sent away to boarding school.
1931	Returns home, attends St. Paul's Girls' School.
1938	Starts degree at Newnham College, Cambridge.
1939	Germany invades Poland; World War II begins.
1941	Earns degree, scholarship, and research grant to work under Ronald Norrish, Professor of Physical Chemistry, Cambridge.
1942	Accepts job at British Coal Utilization Research Association (BCURA) to work on war-related coal research.
1945	Earns PhD in physical chemistry; war ends.
1947	Moves to Paris to work at the Laboratoire Central des Services Chimiques de l'Etat; learns X-ray diffraction techniques from Jacques Mering, becomes an authority on industrial physiochemistry.
1951	Moves back to London, uses X-ray crystallography techniques on DNA at King's College.
1952	Takes "Photo 51;" offered by J. D. Bernal to transfer fellowship to Birkbeck College, London.
1953	Begins work at Birkbeck College using X-ray

diffraction techniques on virus structures; Watson & Crick publish discovery of DNA structure in *Nature* with supporting papers by Franklin and Gosling.

1954 Joined at Birkbeck by Aaron Klug; gathers a small team of researchers who study the tobacco mosaic virus.

1956 Diagnosed with ovarian cancer; continues research; asked to create large scale models and explanations of work on virus structures for display at the Brussels World's Fair.

1957 Begins research on the polio virus.

1958 Dies on April 16 of ovarian cancer.

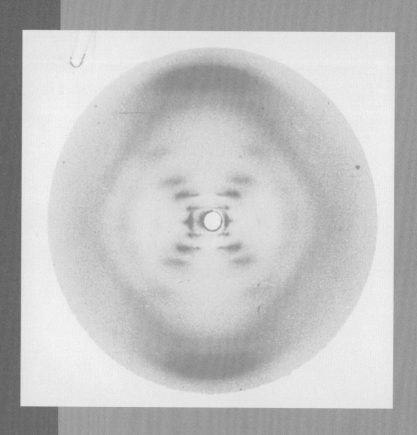

SOURCES

CHAPTER ONE: Early Years

p. 11, "The instant I . . ." James D. Watson, *The Double Helix: A Personal Account of the Discovery of the Structure of DNA* (New York: Scribner, 1968), 167.

p. 11-12, "The pattern was . . ." Ibid., 167-168.

p. 18, "We spent the whole . . ." Jenifer Glynn, "Rosalind Franklin 1920 - 1958," in *Cambridge Women: Twelve Portraits,* ed. Carmen Blacker and Edward Shils (Cambridge: Cambridge University Press, 1996), 270.

p. 18, "Rosalind and I . . ." Brenda Maddox, *Rosalind Franklin: The Dark Lady of DNA* (New York: Harper-Collins, 2002), 28.

p. 18, "A very private . . ." Anne Piper, "Light on a Dark Lady," *Trends in Biochemical Sciences.* 23, no. 4 (1998): 151.

CHAPTER TWO: Young Researcher

p. 25, "Apart from your letters . . ." Maddox, *Rosalind Franklin*, 50.

p. 28, "Science for me . . ." Glynn, *Cambridge Women*, 272.

p. 29, "You look at science . . ." Maddox, *Rosalind Franklin*, 60-61.

p. 30, "Practically the whole . . ." Ibid., 63.

p. 31, "science for money" Ibid., 77.

p. 33, "I don't know whether . . ." Ibid., 73.

p. 33, "extremely kind, good . . ." Ibid., 76.

p. 34, "When I stood up . . ." Ibid., 72.

p. 34, "Miles from anything . . ." Glynn, *Cambridge Women*, 274.

p. 36, "holes in coal" Maddox, *Rosalind Franklin,* 83.

p. 38, "One day we had . . ." Piper, "Light on a Dark Lady," 152.

p. 39, "He's merely expressed . . ." Maddox, *Rosalind Franklin,* 82.

p. 39, "In spite of persistent . . ." Glynn, *Cambridge Women,* 276.

p. 41, "I am quite sure . . ." Maddox, *Rosalind Franklin,* 84.

CHAPTER THREE: Life in Paris

p. 44, "I've been told . . ." Maddox, *Rosalind Franklin,* 92.

p. 45, "Of course my standard . . ." Ibid., 91.

p. 47, "Something happened to Ros . . ." Ibid., 97.

CHAPTER FOUR: Friction and Diffraction

p. 59, "Vacant stupid faces . . ." Maddox, *Rosalind Franklin,* 113.

p. 62, "The PhD slave boy . . ." Anne Sayre, *Rosalind Franklin and DNA* (New York: Norton, 1975), 101.

p. 66, "I proceeded to forget . . ." Watson, *The Double Helix,* 35.

p. 68, "Go back to . . ." Maurice Wilkins, *The Third Man of the Double Helix* (New York: Oxford University Press, 2003), 142.

p. 68, "Why should she . . ." Ibid.

p. 69-70, "felt frustrated . . ." Ibid., 155.

p. 71, "At this time . . ." Watson, *The Double Helix,* 15.

p. 71, "To my surprise . . ." Ibid., 162.

CHAPTER FIVE: Photo 51

p. 73, "It would not . . ." Maddox, *Rosalind Franklin,* 152.

p. 74, "among the most beautiful . . ." Ibid., 308.

p. 77, "Pauling's accomplishment . . ." Watson, *The Double Helix,* 50-51.

p. 79, "That's very nice . . . " Ibid., 162.

p. 80, "known enough chemistry . . ." Ibid., 165.

p. 85, "We spent *ages* . . ." Maddox, *Rosalind Franklin,* 183.

p. 85, "It is with great . . ." Wilkins, *The Third Man of the Double Helix*, 182.

CHAPTER SIX: The Double Helix

p. 87, "a general offensive . . ." Wilkins, *The Third Man of the Double Helix*, 210.

p. 90-91, "an incessant falsetto . . ." Erwin Chargaff, interview by Cold Spring Harbor Laboratory, *DNA Interactive*, 2003, http://www.dnai.org/a/index.html (accessed May 16, 2006).

p. 92, "Linus was . . ." James Watson, interview by Cold Spring Harbor Laboratory, *DNA Interactive*, 2003, http://www.dnai.org/a/index.html (accessed May 16, 2006).

p. 92, "temporarily lost his marbles" Peter Pauling, interview by Cold Spring Harbor Laboratory, *DNA Interactive*, 2003, http://www.dnai.org/a/index.html (accessed May 16, 2006).

p. 92, "drink a toast . . ." Watson, *The Double Helix*, 163.

p. 93, "Suddenly Rosy came . . ." Ibid., 166.

p. 97, "I didn't like . . .", James Watson, interview by Cold Spring Harbor Laboratory, *DNA Interactive*, 2003, http://www.dnai.org/a/index.html (accessed May 16, 2006).

p. 98, "All the hydrogen . . ." Watson, *The Double Helix*, 196.

p. 100, "I think you will . . ." Wilkins, *The Third Man of the Double Helix*, 210.

p. 101, "When you looked . . ." Raymond Gosling, interview by Robyn Williams, *The Science Show, Radio National*, ABC, April 26, 2006. www.abc.net.au/rn/science/ss/stories/s833226.htm (accessed May 16, 2006).

p. 101, "The structure is . . ." Francis Crick, "The Double Helix: A Personal View," *Nature* 248, no. 5451 (April 26, 1974): 766.

p. 103, "It has not escaped . . ." James Watson and Francis

Crick, "Molecular Structure of Nucleic Acids," *Nature* 171, no. 4356 (April 25, 1953): 738.

p. 104, "The previously published . . . " Ibid.

p. 104, "We are much . . ." Ibid.

p. 104, "Let's face it . . ." Maddox, *Rosalind Franklin,* 204.

p. 105, "I do not remember . . ." Glynn, *Cambridge Women,* 280.

CHAPTER SEVEN: A Life Cut Short

p. 106, "a palace to . . ." Maddox, *Rosalind Franklin,* 217.

p. 107, "Eighth century Romanian . . ." Ibid., 218.

p. 110-111, "My lab visits . . ." Ibid., 243.

p. 111, "The centre of Hollywood . . ." Ibid., 246.

p. 113, "She was prickly . . ." Ibid., 255.

p. 113, "I would have . . ." Ibid.

p. 113, "She *noticed* . . . ." Sayre, *Rosalind Franklin,* 178.

p. 114, "you do not disapprove . . ." Maddox, *Rosalind Franklin*, 252.

p. 117, "more rapport with . . ." Ibid., 265.

p. 119, "The size of a . . ." Ibid., 285.

p. 124, "You'll never guess . . ." Ibid., 298.

CHAPTER EIGHT: The Last Word

p. 128, "discoveries concerning the . . ." Nobelprize.org, "The Nobel Prize in Physiology or Medicine in 1962," Nobel Foundation, http://nobelprize.org/medicine/laureates/1962/ (accessed May 16, 2006).

p. 131, "It was Rosalind . . ." Aaron Klug, "From Macromolecules to Biological Assemblies," (Nobel Lecture, Stockholm, Sweden, December 8, 1982). http://nobelprize.org/chemistry/laureates/1982/klug-lecture.pdf (accessed May 16, 2006).

p. 132, "golden hands" Maddox, *Rosalind Franklin*, 95.

BIBLIOGRAPHY

Crick, Francis. "The Double Helix: A Personal View" *Nature* 248, no. 5451 (April 26, 1974): 766-69.

Erwin Chargaff, "Erwin Chargaff; The Meeting with Watson and Crick," interview by Cold Spring Harbor Laboratory, *DNA Interactive*, 2003, http://www.dnai.org/a/index.html (accessed May 16, 2006).

Glynn, Jenifer. "Rosalind Franklin 1920 –1958." In *Cambridge Women: Twelve Portraits*, edited by Carmen Blacker and Edward Shils, 267-82. Cambridge, UK: Cambridge University Press, 1996.

James Watson, "James Watson and Francis Crick; Base Pairing," interview by Cold Spring Harbor Laboratory, *DNA Interactive*, 2003, http://www.dnai.org/a/index.html. (accessed May 16, 2006).

James Watson, "Linus Pauling; Would Pauling Correct His Mistake?," interview by Cold Spring Harbor Laboratory, *DNA Interactive*, 2003, http://www.dnai.org/a/index.html (accessed May 16, 2006).

Klug, Aaron. "From Macromolecules to Biological Assemblies," Nobel Lecture, http://nobelprize.org/chemistry/laureates/1982/klug-lecture.pdf (accessed May 16, 2006).

Maddox, Brenda. *Rosalind Franklin: The Dark Lady of DNA*. New York: HarperCollins, 2002.

Nobelprize.org, "The Nobel Prize in Physiology or Medicine in 1962," Nobel Foundation, http://nobelprize.org/medicine/laureates/1962/ (accessed August 16, 2006).

Peter Pauling, "Linus Pauling; The Triple Helix," interview by Cold Spring Harbor Laboratory, *DNA Interactive*, 2003, http://www.dnai.org/a/index.html (accessed May 16, 2006).

Piper, Anne. "Light on a Dark Lady," *Trends in Biochemical Sciences*, 23, no. 4 (1998), 151-54.

Raymond Gosling, "The Dark Lady of DNA; A Portrait of Rosalind Franklin," interview by Lynne Malcolm and Robyn Williams. *The Science Show, Radio National*, ABC (April 26, 2003). http://www.abc.net.au/rn/science/ss/stories/s833226.htm (accessed May 16, 2006).

Sayre, Anne. *Rosalind Franklin and DNA*. New York: Norton, 1975.

Watson, James D. *The Double Helix: A Personal Account of the Discovery of the Structure of DNA*. New York: Scribner, 1998.

Watson, James and Francis Crick. "Molecular Structure of Nucleic Acids," *Nature* 171, no. 4356 (April 25, 1953): 737-38.

Wilkins, Maurice. *The Third Man of the Double Helix*. New York: Oxford University Press, 2003.

WEB SITES

http://www.dnai.org/
The Cold Spring Harbor Laboratory maintains this extensive site dedicated to DNA and features many topics related to the discovery of DNA, including interviews, videos, games, and animation.

http://cwp.library.ucla.edu/
The site, entitled Contributions of 20th Century Women to Physics, offers an archive composed of female scientists throughout history, including a detailed section dedicated to Rosalind Franklin.

http://www.pbs.org/wgbh/nova/photo51/
PBS's NOVA series offers a Web site dedicated exclusively to Rosalind Franklin and her famous discovery. It features a useful article that details the famous Photo 51 and provides illustrated instructions on how to decipher the image.

http://www.royalsociety.ac.uk/page.asp?tip=1&id=1782
The Royal Society in the United Kingdom offers the annual Royal Society Rosalind Franklin Award to scientists with outstanding achievements. Visit this site to learn more about this award and its past recipients.

INDEX

Franklin, Colin (brother), 14, 16, 23, 25-26, 81
Franklin, David (brother), 14, 16, 23, 25-26
Franklin, Ellis (father), 13-19, 22-23, 25-29, 38-39, 45, 58, 63, 120, 124
Franklin, Irene (cousin), 37-38
Franklin, Jenifer (sister), 14-16, 25-26, 32, 105, 123
Franklin, Muriel (mother), 13-14, 16-19, 25-26, 38-39, 45, 58, 120, 124
Franklin, Roland (brother), 14, 16, 23, 25-26, 33
Franklin, Rosalind Elise, *10, 15, 40, 46, 50, 123, 131*
at BCURA, 35-42
at Birkbeck College, 106-126
birth, 13-14
death, 126
education, 16-19, 22-25, 27-28, 30-34
first trip to America, 109-111
illness, 119-126
at King's College, 58-71, 42-86, 87-97
second trip to America, 116-119

Franklin, Ursula (cousin), 18, 47, 125
Fraser, Bruce, 79-80

Gosling, Raymond, 60, 62, 64-65, 69, 80, 83-86, 87, 93, 101-103
Griffith, John, 89, 98

Hitler, Adolf, 19-20, 25, 28-29
Holmes, Kenneth, 112-113

Kerslake, Jean, 18-19, 38-40
King's College, London, 53-54, 58-59, *59,* 60, 62, 64-66, 71-72, 73-74, 76-82, 85, 87, 90-94, 96-97, 101, 103-106, 107, 111-113, 131
Klug, Aaron, 111-113, *112,* 116, 124, 128, 130-131

Laboratorie des Services Chimiques de l'Etat, 43-54
Luzzati, Denise, 47, 123
Luzzati, Vittorio, 46-47, 82, 123, 132

Mathieu, Marcel, 41
Medical Research Council (MRC), 53, 60-61, 71, 81,